Food

Book & Journal

Candice Jones

First Edition.

Publisher: Living With More Publications

Cover Design: Candice Gilgore

Scriptures were taken from various versions of the HOLY BIBLE.

ISBN: 978-0-578-41242-9

Simply and Sincerely Grateful

Thank you, Holy Spirit for without you this book wouldn't be! You are the battery in my back and the fire in my soul!

I want to acknowledge and sincerely thank, Dr. Joseph and Eva Rodriguez of Agape Faith Bible Training Center in Birch Run, MI., and Pastor Autwan and Lady Kim Roland of New Harvest Church. It is because of you all that I undoubtedly know the powerful force of faith and the activating ability of my words. I am a whosoever that can have whatsoever! I am eternally grateful! I dedicate this book to all of you.

Thank you to my husband, my best friend, my everything! Thank you for allowing me the time, gifting me the support, and always believing in my God dreams! For your sacrifice there are no words, so I will simply and sincerely say thank you.

Thank you, Dad, Pastor Dennis K. Hutchins, I am confident that you will forever be my biggest supporter and greatest influencer. Thank you for your leadership. I love you beyond anything I can articulate with mere words.

My three heartbeats, Linston Isiah Jones IV, Cameron Keith Jones, and Carsten Kole Jones, you all continue to be my driving motivation and inspiration. My earnest prayer is that you continue to grow and be strong in the Lord and always use your faith and words to speak life! Thank you for inspiring mommy in ways no one else could ever do.

Thank you to Apostle Latrice Williams for being my Destiny Driver! Thank you, Lakita Corey "twin" for your prayers, love, and support. My village (Rasheeda, Richole, Connie and family) I'm grateful to do this thing called life with you all! My heart is full and I'm truly grateful we are on this journey together. Thanks for always being my support system, prayer partners, and everything between. I love you deeply.

Thank you to those who continue to speak life into me Bishop Derrick W. Hutchins, Pastor Phonz, and Bishop Alvernis Johnson.

AUTHOR'S CONTACT INFO

Website:
www.candicejones.com

Email:
contact@candicejones.com

Facebook:
https://www.facebook.com/foodforfaith14/

Instagram:
www.instagram.com/foodforfaith14

Introduction

Initially, I didn't set out to write a book or a devotional. I was really, just trying to survive. My heart's desire was to mature in my calling, grow spiritually, and simply know God in a more intimate way. I wanted to attend Bible college and God Himself orchestrated it perfectly so that I could. I knew He was calling me to a higher level. I knew the gently tug in my spirit saying, "*come closer daughter*," was His loving voice. His voice was enticing to my spirit and I thirst and hungered for him more than anything else. As a deer pants for flowing streams, so pants my soul for you, O God. My soul was longing for more of God and less of me.

I didn't just want Him, I wanted to share Him...share His love and His Gospel in a more effective way. I wanted to be equipped for His use and His glory. I knew I needed to sit under good, sound teaching and grow spiritually. I knew it wouldn't be easy, but I was ready. Ha! Or, at least I thought I was ready. I knew it would be a sacrifice, but I was committed. I knew it would require discipline, time, money, and some effort on my part, but I was determined.

I was working full-time and a full-time student when I started. I was also a mom, a minister, a wife, a sister, and a friend. I thought I knew the magnitude of the sacrifice that going and studying the Word of God would cost me. Boy, was I wrong! I was completely clueless of the consequences of my commitment to those three years in Bible College. Because of my drive and pure determination to know God and make Him known, the enemy of my soul seemed to place a target on my back and started shooting. He was aiming to kill, and you couldn't tell me that I wasn't on his hit list.

His fiery darts started coming. I am sure they were always coming at me, but they seemed to be intensified. I started to experience attacks in every area of my life. My relationships were under attack - marriage, friendships, even professional ones! My health! My mind! My finances! My career! My kids! Nothing seemed to be off limits. Wait! Was this in the admissions paperwork? Did I miss some fine print? Or, had my determination to grow spiritually pissed the devil off?

So, how did this book or manual come to life? For three years, every Thursday night from 6 - 9pm, I attended Faith Agape Bible Training Center, in Saginaw, MI. My professor taught on faith every third hour - yep for all three years. I thought I know all there was to know about faith. After all, I was a church kid, a preachers' kid (PK), a faithful bible study attendee, a Christian, and a Minister of the gospel. I knew that faith was the substance of things hoped for and the evidence of things not seen according to Hebrews 11:1. Wasn't that enough?

Couldn't I just throw that scripture at the enemy when he came for me? I quickly learned it wasn't sufficient! It is one thing to have a gun, it is a completely different thing to know how to use it. I was throwing bullets at the enemy without the force and impact of a weapon. Bullets aren't deadly without a gun. I had been deceived! Christians are ineffective without the Holy Spirit, the Fruit of the Spirit, and Faith! Knowing scripture wasn't going to be enough. It was going to require faith in what I knew. The church hadn't taught me enough about my God given faith and how to use it to get the God kind of results I desperately needed in my life. I didn't know the operation of Faith. I didn't know how it worked or what it even sounded like.

I didn't have the revelation of Mark 11:23 - the operation of faith. That scripture really tells us that speaking is even more important than believing. I didn't understand that it would take much more than me just believing the Bible to stop the fiery darts of the enemy from consuming me.

You mean, I have to open my mouth and say something? I must speak it to see it? Every week I learned more and more about my authority as a believer. That knowledge began to spark excitement, determination, and drive I didn't know existed in my soul. It truly becomes like fire shut up in your bones. I couldn't wait to open my eyes in the morning and start forming my day with my words. Yes, my words worked! I could defeat the enemy of my soul with my words! Really?!

But, as fast as I learned - the darts were coming equally as fast. It was as if the enemy knew I was becoming dangerously armed with faith filled declarations from the Word of God and they were all aimed at his head! I had to learn how to use what I was learning quickly, and I needed to see immediate results. I would love to tell you that manifestation came rushing in like a mighty wind, but that was not my reality. As I learned the sound of faith, the voice of faith, its rhythm and how to use it - I begin to slowly see manifestation. And each year, the more I use my faith muscle, the stronger it gets and the quicker I see results.

People often say that faith is like a muscle. So, how do we strengthen that faith muscle? We exercise it! Especially when we least feel like it. As the enemy began to attack me in different areas of my life, I began to fight back. I have never been much of a fighter. I have always had sisters that would jump in and fight for me, often before I could ever get a word in. But when it comes to the devil and all his little demons, I had to learn how to fight for myself. Others can only cover you for so long. At some point, you have to fight! It became easier as I realized that all of heaven was backing me when I used the right weapons.

My faith filled words were sending angels to war on my behalf. We must become skilled in our warfare, knowing that our weapons are not carnal but mighty through God to the pulling down of strongholds (2 Corinthians 10:4 KJV). We must become skilled in speaking those things that be not as though they were. Skilled at being unwavering in our faith confession! Skilled at saying it until we see it. Repetition is the mother of all skill - so just keep saying it.

Our lack of consistency is what the enemy is counting on to count us out. It is only through consistency that we see results. I had to become consistent in what I was believing and speaking before I expected to consistently receive from heaven. We must be stable in our confession. The bible talks about the double - minded man and how he shouldn't expect anything from God. We must become and remain firm, focused, and unshakable in our declarations. We must speak intentional words, full of power, and expect them to produce. Mountains will move! Giants will fall! Sickness will go! All of this at the response of our words.

We have an advantage that we often fail to utilize. That advantage is the Person of the Holy Spirit. He is the greater one in us working through us. Yes, He is our secret weapon - a sneak attack! See, the enemy doesn't fight fair and neither should we. When our words are thrust out by the power of the Holy Spirit, the enemy takes a mighty blow of destruction. That blow dismantles every plot, plan, and scheme he has for our lives. Knowing that, I learned to speak life before I saw death.

I was becoming strategic at sabotaging his schemes, identifying his tricks, and frustrating his plans before they were ever exposed. Speaking before he attacked was like putting money in the bank before I needed to withdraw it. It was insurance! Just in case you're coming for my health, let me speak healing! Just in case you decide to come for my family today, let me speak protection. Just in case you decide to try to steal my peace and sanity, let me go ahead and release the peace of God over every atmosphere before I step into it.

We must be consistent and relentless in our speaking. Not passive and nonchalant - but forceful in our speaking. The bible says in Matthew 11:12, "the kingdom of God has suffered violent assault but the energetic take it by force." Are you suffering violent assault? Is the enemy coming hard for you and your family? You have to get mad enough to fight back. There is simply no victory without opposition! That simply means, there is not a victory without a fight! This isn't a fight that passivity will win. You need the supernatural energy and anointing of God to speak words that will cut the throat of the enemy.

Oh no, we are not playing nice! Wrong book ma'am! We are after the enemy's head, because he is playing with our minds, our marriages and families, our money, and our very destinies. This is a faith fight so put your earrings back on and put the Vaseline away. God is throwing the blows as we release our words! Heavens army of Angels is ready to war at our command.

Wow, that is so powerful! All of heaven responds to our faith. Our faith is downright captivating, magnetic, and irresistible to our great God. It's the only thing He responds to. Our faith is irresistible to him and indefensible to the enemy. So, when we want to fight the enemy, we fight with the shield of faith, extinguishing all he throws at us. Glory!

Understand that God is drawn to our situations when we release His Word with His faith. Counterfeit faith won't do! Only acceptable faith, the God kind of faith, will produce good fruit. What are your producing with your words? He deposited His faith in us at salvation and even before. It took faith for us to believe there was a God and to accept His son Jesus as our Lord and Savior. We have all been given the measure of faith according to Romans 12:3 which says, "For I say, through the grace given unto me, to every man that is among you, not to think *of himself* more highly than he ought to think; but to think soberly, according as God hath dealt to every man the measure of faith." (KJV) God gave us just what we needed to get His attention, provision, and intervention. He gave us acceptable faith!

As women, we can be a bit emotional at times. Ok, I will just speak for myself. I can be a bit emotional at times. I would get angry at God when He didn't respond to my tears and emotional tantrums. I was kicking and screaming to get my way. Did He not see me? Did He care? Did my tears mean anything to Him? He is our father! He hears and cares about everything that concerns us. But He is a God of principles. And His faith principle remains the same regardless of our emotional breakdowns.

His Word says we can have what we say in Mark 11:23. Not what we cry about! Not what we feel entitled to. Not what we feel the enemy stole from us. Not even what we labored for. We *shall* have what we say and what you say you shall have! That simple. So, get up, stop kicking and screaming and start speaking.

When you look at Mark 11:23, He requires us to speak even more than he demands we believe.

Mark 11:23 KJV For verily I say unto you, that whosoever shall say unto this mountain, be thou removed, and be thou cast into the sea; and shall not doubt in his heart, but shall believe that those things which he saith shall come to pass; he shall have whatsoever he saith.

He says "SAY OR SAITH" three times in this scripture and believe once.

Speaking must be pretty critical to this process, huh? Here's the thing - if you say it enough, you *will* believe it. Like many of you, I was tired of being tired, sick of being sick...you know the rest. I was doing all I knew how to do, and that wasn't enough. I had no clue how to release my faith and get what I needed from the invisible realm to the realm I was stuck in - which at times felt a lot like hell! I was trapped in that realm because of lack of knowledge. I didn't realize that faith was the only acceptable currency to make an exchange with God. He had everything I needed, and I was frustrated that He wasn't releasing it to me.

My tears were extremely effective on my earthly daddy. But, my heavenly Father wasn't rewarding my tears. If my daddy, being a man, knows how to give good gifts, how much more does my Father in Heaven know how to release every good and perfect thing to me? Why was my heavenly Father withholding things from me?

I knew He loved me and wanted to release what I needed to me. But -nothing! I was beyond agitated that the "Good God" wasn't being "good" to me. What I didn't realize was that me not receiving what I needed or desired from God, was more about me and not Him. He doesn't change; He remains the same. He is a good, good Father. It was me! I was the problem! I wasn't releasing the very thing He deposited in me to receive what was available! Healing, prosperity, peace - all of these were available! I was just unlearned and suffering as a result.

I thank God for Dr. Joseph and Eva Rodriguez. They taught me that God is good, and His mercy endures forever. I learned that my good God wants all my needs and desires met, but He needs my faith to do it. Faith is the ingredient we must contribute to God's recipes.

You mean, I have something that I can offer to God that He can use? What!? Yes, our faith is eagerly anticipated by our Father. He is waiting on us to release it.

Bible College changed my life for so many reasons. But, there are two things I learned that I'm so grateful to now know.

First, faith comes by hearing *and* hearing *and* hearing *and* hearing *and* hearing the Word of God. Romans 10:17 says – So, then faith *comes* by hearing, and hearing by the word of God.

That word *hearing* is a continuous state of hearing. We must position ourselves to always be hearing the Word of God to strengthen our faith. Our faith is fueled by the Word of God alone, and it must be fed by it continuously. Here is my warning - once you feed your faith a five-star meal, it will never be satisfied with drive through experiences. Meat is meat and there is no substitute for meat. Nothing else will do.

The second thing I learned during this process was - the Word of God is more effective at fueling your faith when it comes from your own mouth. You have to eat your own cooking. You have to eat the Word of God, released from your own mouth. Speak over yourself! Encourage yourself in the Lord! Open your own mouth and declare some things, and what *YOU* declare, will be established for *YOU*. **Job 22:28 NKJV** says - "You will also declare a thing, and it will be established for you; So light will shine on your ways."

I made it through the three years of bible college and many other hard times. I overcame sleepless nights, dry seasons, and dead situations by learning to speak life regardless of what I saw with my natural eyes. As my professor would often say - if I can see, touch, taste, or hear it, it is subject to change. Let me break that down for you. When something is subject to change, a date for example, that means we shouldn't get too comfortable with it. It's conditional, not firm. It's tentative, not carved in stone. It reminds me of when Jesus went and called Lazarus from his temporary dead situation.

EVERYTHING has to respond and change when Jesus speaks. That's good! So, let me help you. "I have been crucified with Christ; and it is no longer I who live, but Christ lives in me; and the life which I now live in the flesh I live by faith in the Son of God, who loved me and gave Himself up for me. (Galatians 2:20) Are you getting this? When you speak from your inner man, Jesus is speaking! So, Christ in us makes us unstoppable. Whatever you're facing today is subject to change over the next 14 days. And that change will only happen if you open your mouth and declare change. It will happen if you open your mouth like Jesus did and call something out from the grave. Call something forth! And "it" - whatever "it" is, will only get better if you learned to speak better.

The more I spoke better, the more I began to think better, and the more things got better. I begin to write faith confessions for areas of my life that were under attack. I would speak those things that were not as though they were in spite of and in the middle of what I was experiencing. My thoughts at first were simply... I'm paying for Bible college, so I might as well see if this stuff really works! I really wasn't sure? But what did I have to lose?

God didn't say I had to 100% believe in my mind. He said believe in my heart and speak it. He said don't doubt in your heart, but that had nothing to do with this mind of mine. The Word of God was renewing my mind as I was being taught. I was just going to go for it!

Yep! People may have thought I had lost my mind! I was decreeing abundance and my bank account said insufficient funds. I was declaring I was healthy, wealthy, and wise, with 10 different prescriptions and living paycheck to paycheck. But I kept speaking.

I started speaking life to people that had been given days to live. I had the audacity to speak life to marriages that were basically in divorce court. I was declaring and decree.

Speaking and believing...well kind of believing. And the craziest thing started to happen. The more I said it, the more I believed it! Then, the more I said it, the more I believed it, the more I saw!

Wait, did I detect a pattern? Does God work on a pattern? Is there a system? Can I master this thing? Say it, believe it, see it? Say it, believe it, see it? Say it, believe it, see it? Ok, God - I see you!

Here's the thing - it is a lot easier to chant the pattern above than it is to actually do it! Believe me, I know. I have felt for a while that God was calling me to share some of my faith declarations outside of social media posts, to really help someone else learn how to fight back. He was calling me to encourage someone to speak life every day and know that you shall have what you say.

Now, wait! Let me qualify somethings. If you are speaking something against the will and plan of God for your life, you must stop immediately! It is a waste of words and energy. Your words will produce, but they will produce your Ishmael! Ishmaels are the results of us trying to make things happen through carnal methods. Christians should be led by the Spirit of God, even - well especially when we are speaking things into existence. This works whether you are led by the Spirit of God or your flesh.

See, even unbelievers know that there is power in their words (a principle is a principle), there are thousands of books on positive affirmation, declaration, and daily confessions. So, the principle of speaking things into existence, works whether you are spiritual or carnal minded. Whether you have the mind of Christ or not, your words will manifest.

But, why produce or birth something that is not the will of God for your life? You'll have to use more words to try to fix it! You can save yourself a whole lot of "fix it Jesus," if you would just speak His will, not yours. The more you pursue God and get to know Him, the more you will speak exactly what is aligned with His will for your life. He will transform your mind, purify your desires, and bind your will to His. You will rejoice in things that make Him rejoice and turn away from things that separate you from Him. In essence, you will speak what is on the heart of the Father concerning you. His thoughts will become your words and those words deliver your destiny.

How to Use This Devotional

Welcome to your new normal! On this 14-day journey, we will speak life to all dead areas. We will curse all unfruitful areas. And we will see the manifestation of it all. I have written you a short letter of encouragement everyday followed by your faith confession for that day.

We will confess what God has already spoken concerning us. We will fill our atmosphere with life altering declaration that will elevate us out of our P.I.T.S (Places Intended to Stop us, Slow us down, Stagnate us, Sabotage us). We will use our faith filled words to overcome places, people, and traps intended to prevent us from entering our God ordained place of purpose and position of power. We will dismantle Satan's work in our lives and the lives of those connected to us. We shall have whatsoever we say!

There are 14 days of declarations and scripture references to meditate on. Joshua 1:8 says - "Keep this Book of the Law always on your lips; meditate on it day and night, so that you may be careful to do everything written in it. Then you will be prosperous and successful." Don't feel like you have to rush to day 14. It can be difficult learning to speak another language, especially as an adult! Try French at 30 years old -

no ma'am! It isn't impossible, but statistically, it is most difficult to learn a new language, the older you get.

So, take it slow but be consistent in your pursuit of Kingdom speaking! Also, if there is an area you are currently experiencing turmoil and attack, stay there! Keep confessing that declaration over and over until Heaven responds! And heaven WILL respond. The bible teaches us in Jeremiah 1:12 that God is watching His Word to perform it (NASB).

These declarations are full of the Word of God for that very reason. We are not on a meaningless mission to magnify our own words, but we are magnifying what God said! Why? Because our words are just words. But, when He speaks, or we speak His words, worlds are formed, stars decorate the sky, people come forth out of graves, winds calm, storms obey, chains break, prisons shake, demons tremble!

His words, not ours! Speak through us God! He is watching and waiting to perform His Word on our behalf; let's put Him to work!

I can imagine God, on the edge of His throne, pleading for us to tag Him in. He wants to be reminded of His words concerning you. He wants to intervene for His daughters. We have to tag Him by speaking His words ONLY to the impossible situations in our life and giving Him a stage to perform.

This is a process, so don't get weary in well doing. Keep speaking. Keep speaking it until you see it! I would encourage you to speak these declarations a few times a day. I really tried to keep them short for that purpose. Write them on an index card and place them in places that you visit several times a day, like your mirror, or in your car, or at your desk. Hey, the enemy isn't taking a break on what he is prophesying over your life and you shouldn't either.

Relentlessness will reward you with results! Make use of the journal entry pages provided for you and get ready to be inspired to write your own declaration as the Holy Spirit leads you. Believe me, once you start speaking faith filled words, you won't want to stop. We were created to speak life, it's in our Kingdom DNA. We were created in the image and with the likeness of God, who created all things with His words. He spoke the world into existence and we can speak with the same power and authority. "Let there be," should be the normal faith talk of a believer. I know it sounds real "God like" and will take some practice. But I dare you to start walking around with a "Let there be" swag in your spirit. Once you realize how powerful your words are, you will not want to shut up!

We will declare what God says about us and about the situations we are facing in our life! We will declare aloud, proud, and confidently that He who has promised is faithful to perform. Perform His word! Demonstrate His power!

This isn't the book that you quietly sit on your comfy chair and sip coffee silently reading. Wrong book! I encourage you to stand somewhere flat footed in your combat boots or red bottoms with your chest out and declare what thus says the Lord each day. I love that scene in the movie "*War Room*" when Priscilla Shirer, who plays the main character Elizabeth Jordan, opens the door, and kicks the devil out of her home with her words. She begins to declare what belonged to her and what the enemy could no longer have. That was such a powerful scene in that movie. She had to make some declarations and put the enemy on notice that his time had expired!

You have to take off the gloves you have been fighting with and open your mouth to fight in God like fashion. You can kick the devil out with our "Let there be" power. Now, that's some real girl power! Let there be peace in your homes. Let there be harmony in your relationships. Let there be divine health in your body. Let there be more than enough in your accounts. Let there be soundness in your minds. Let there be light in every dark area in your life. Let there be...hallelujah!

We kick our adversary out by speaking. He must get out of our homes, out of our minds, out of our finances, and out of our children. We are pretty and powerful my sister, and we are getting ready to tap into the power of our words. We will use our authority that has been given to the believer coupled with our God given faith and speak those things we want to see. Go ahead and release this into the atmosphere now - "I shall have exactly what I say."

Lastly, don't work against your confessions with negatives words. Thoughts will come but you decide what will stay! Cast down imaginations and every high thing that exalts itself against the knowledge of God and bring into captivity every thought to the obedience of Christ (2 Corinthians 10:5).

Oh yeah - speak life or shut up! All I can say is get ready! If you stay on this journey with me, I know you will see the goodness of our great God. Our consistent, faith filled words will produce manifestation!

Day 1

"I discovered the more I say what God says about me, the less I remember what people have said."

Hey Beautiful,

Question? If I asked you to think of one-word God would use to describe you, what would you say? Or, if I ask what He has spoken concerning you, would you know? Would anything even erupt out of your spirit? If I asked you what people have said concerning you, I'm sure like me, you would be able to quote it all verbatim!

What He says about us should flow out of us like explosive volcanic eruptions, completely consuming all other words spoken over us, about us, or to us. In this world, we are constantly surrounded and consumed by so many superficial things and yes, even shallow people who dare to define us with their words. We are drowning in unrealistic expectations of who we should be, what we should sound like, and what we should look like.

It's oh so easy to forget who and whose we are. We often take on labels and limitations that people place on us. We have allowed society, social media, television, and even church and family to dictate how we should look, sound, and dress. All resulting in our lack of confidence, demise of our uniqueness, and destruction of all authenticity.

We change our hair, clothes, and social media statuses to fit into a world that we were never created to blend into. We master wearing masks to appear worthy of acceptance on the outside, while our insides are in desperate need of alterations.

We value the opinions and words of others more than the words and thoughts of the One who created us. Sometimes, we allow people who aren't even close to us, to determine our worth and value. We are also guilty of devaluing ourselves when we look at ourselves through the lens of hurt, betrayal, disappointment, and failure. We must see ourselves through the lens of Christ. Only a creator really knows the purpose and true value of His creation.

Why do we allow the words of people to be the pencils that sketch our self-portraits? That was me! I was always adjusting who I was based on the thoughts and words of people. I was trying to be perfect for imperfect people; desperately needing to "fit in" instead of "stand out," like my Daddy created me to do.

Then I started to study what God, my Creator, said about me and started to meditate on that. I learned a powerful solution to take that pencil back and I want to empower you to do the same. I discovered the more I say what God says about me, the less I remember what people have said! Thank God pencil can be erased, even to the degree that you don't see a glimpse of what was there. See, only Jesus has the permanent ink of His blood, therefore, only what He says is permanent in my life. He determined my worth when He went to Calvary and shed His blood for me. So, I choose to speak His words, His thoughts, His work, and His love for me.

Let's start speaking what God says about us ONLY, until it transforms our self-portrait into the beautiful image God created; until our interior matches our beautiful exterior.

Here's your declaration for today. Say it until it takes root in your spirit! Say it until the woman in the mirror, looking back at you, is full of confidence and immeasurable self-worth! Say it until you see yourself as fearfully and wonderfully made by the Creator of all things good and perfect!

Scriptures for Meditation:

Psalm 139:14 KJV - I will praise thee; for I am fearfully and wonderfully made: marvelous are thy works; and that my soul knoweth right well.

Ephesians 2:10 NIV - For we are God's handiwork, created in Christ Jesus to do good works, which God prepared in advance for us to do.

Job 33:4 NIV - The Spirit of God has made me; the breath of the Almighty gives me life.

Declaration
I Am What God Says and Only That

I am the marvelous handiwork of God. A masterpiece uniquely designed to bring glory to God. I am fearfully and wonderfully made by the Creator of the heavens and earth. His Spirit created me, His thoughts have defined me, His hands have shaped and molded me, and His very breath gave me life.

I am His artwork - truly perfect and uniquely designed. In Christ, I am a daughter of the Most High God - the King of kings. I have been adopted into His royal family. I am a chosen daughter, a royal priesthood - God's very own special possession.

I am loved by Him! I am valuable to Him! My value can only be determined by God and He thought I was worth dying for, getting up for, and ascending for. He counted me worthy of His son! I am the apple of His eye, and because He delights in me, He saved me.

I bring Him great pleasure. He made me the salt of the earth and the light of the world to stand out, not to fit in. He placed His spirit on the inside of me and entrusts me with His glory.

I am a glory carrier; anointed and appointed for such a time as this.

I am great because the greater One resides in me. I am beautiful because He Himself designed me for a special purpose. I am unique because He makes no duplicates. I am significant to the plan of God. I am valuable to the Kingdom of God.

I am pretty and powerful, armed, and dangerous to the Kingdom of darkness. God has made me with the same hands that placed the stars in the sky, made the seas, and that formed the dry land. Marvelous are His works! He delights in all the works of His hand!

I am His handiwork! Today, I will see myself as God does!

Continue Your Declaration Here:

Day 2

"Speak those things that be not as though they were and watch the "SUDDENLY" begin to erupt in your life."

Hey Beautiful,

Did you know that in your innermost being flows rivers of living water? Now, that ought to shout you right there! We have living waters inside of us! Open your mouth and release that living water and drown the enemy of your soul. The enemy can't kill, steal, or destroy you, when you open your mouth and release living water. That water only comes from depositing God's Word in your spirit. Living water only comes from the Word of a Living God.

You have living water, healing words, destroying power, cancelling authority, wall collapsing sound, ceiling breaking POWER - all in your mouth. How dare you remain silent? I command your spirit to speak up! You have the ability to change your situation and situations of others. You house the authority to shift atmospheres. Your words can shake everything around you and cause the "suddenly" and "immediate" things of God to occur.

Spectators will say "she was broke, busted and disgusted...but suddenly." She was depressed...but suddenly! She was sick unto death...but suddenly. Her marriage was failing...but suddenly. She couldn't have children...but suddenly.

You will testify, "I declared it and immediately it manifested." Speak those things that be not as though they were and watch the "*SUDDENLY*" begin to erupt in your life. Today, we are declaring that we are free indeed from all condemnation, shame, and guilt and suddenly - it shall be so!

Those tactics of the enemy have kept us bound long enough. God isn't mad at us. He corrects us in love, because we are His children, but He never imprisons us to our past. I'm reminded of Peter, being imprisoned and while the church was praying and interceding for him…the suddenly happened on his behalf.

I declare this declaration will cause you to be liberated suddenly, from condemnation, shame, and guilt. Whom the Son sets free is free! You are free and free indeed! Indeed - means without questions. Stop answering to people questioning your freedom when the God who forgave you has no questions about the matter.

Free Indeed!! Be Free! Let's declare our freedom!

Scripture Meditation:

John 8:36 KJV If the Son therefore shall make you free, ye shall be free indeed.

Romans 8:1 NIV Therefore, there is now no condemnation for those who are in Christ Jesus.

1 John 1:9 KJV If we confess our sins, He is faithful and just to forgive us our sins, and to cleanse us from all unrighteousness.

Declaration

I am Forgiven and Free Indeed

Today, I am forgiven and free from every trick and trap of condemnation the enemy has orchestrated against me. I am the righteousness of God, through Christ Jesus. All condemnation is cancelled by the liberating Word of God over my life.

I am free from shame and the residue of my past. My past doesn't have a permanent place in my present or future. My past doesn't disqualify me for destiny. I will not drown in the failures, disappointments, hurt, pain, guilt, or shame of my past. I will not allow people to remind me of who I use to be; I will walk fully in who I am today.

I am righteous! I am holy! I am loved! I am free!

Every chain was broken on the cross and I receive my inheritance of freedom. Jesus purchased my freedom with an overpayment of His precious blood. He who knew no sin, took mine, so that I could be free. I refuse to be bound. Everything that could hold me captive, Jesus led to captivity!

I am free from every curse of the law. I am not a slave to sin. I will not be imprisoned by people! Jesus redeemed me! His blood set me free! His presence keeps me liberated.

Every chain of bondage must break off me now. I am walking into my day, in the presence of God, totally forgiven and free. Free to live out loud! Free to pursue my purpose! Free to be who He called me to be! Free to operate in every gift, mantle, and office He has called me to.

Free to love! Free to forgive! Free to try again! Free to worship! Free to pray! Free to be in his presence!

I am free and free indeed!

Continue Your Declaration Here:

____

____

____

____

____

Day 3

"Your faith will only rise to the level of your own confession of the Word of God."

Hey Beautiful,

I can do all things through Christ is hard to believe right? Here's the thing - you will never believe what you aren't willing to speak. Faith comes by hearing! Your faith will only rise to the level of your own confession of the Word of God. Simply put, you have to say it before you see it! And boy do I want you to see it.

David said in **Psalm 27:13 NIV**, "I remain confident of this: I will see the goodness of the LORD in the land of the living." I want you to see the goodness of our Lord and Savior. He has so much goodness for us, but He requires substance (matter, material) called faith - our faith. He needs your faith filled words as ingredients to create the God-kind-of-life you are promised in His Word.

Jesus said, "The thief cometh not but for to steal, and to kill and to destroy; I am come that you might have life, and that they might have it more abundantly." **(John 10:10 KJV)** That abundant life is on the other side of your declaration. You must DECLARE a thing for it to be established. **(Job 22:28 NKJV)** To declare means to make known, to state clearly or to announce officially. Establish means to set up on a firm or permanent basis, to show to be valid or true. Are you getting this?

What you announce and make known will be permanently set up and will prove to be true!! Wow - the authority God has given to the believer! Yes, you and I have the power and authority to speak things and they will be legally established based on our rank in the Kingdom. We can have all the power and authority available to man according to Matthew 16:19, Luke 10:19-21, Mark 16:17, James 4:7-9 **KJV**...but because we refuse to open our mouths and exercise that power, nothing will change!

You have to speak to make something known! You must SAY to the mountain - be cast into the sea before it is removed. You must say mountain of fear – Go! Mountain of doubt – Go! Mountain of sickness - Go! Whatever mountain or wall that is blocking you from entering your promised place, I dare you to command it to GO!

Speak up, woman of God! Daughter of Zion, Declare! Decree! Proclaim! Prophesy! Speak!

You must SPEAK those things that be not, as though there were, before they are. You must declare something before something is established. Yes absolutely, you can do all things through Christ!

Speak it! Make it known until you and your enemies know it is so...and so shall it be!

Scripture Meditation

Philippians 4:13 NKJV I can do all things through Christ who strengthens me.

Daniel 11:32b KJV ... but the people that do know their God shall be strong and do exploits.

Mark 9:22 KJV Jesus said unto him, "If thou canst believe, all things are possible to him that believeth."

Matthew 17:20 KJV And Jesus said unto them, Because of your unbelief: for verily I say unto you, if ye have faith as a grain of mustard seed, ye shall say unto this mountain, remove hence to yonder place; and it shall remove; and nothing shall be impossible unto you.

Ephesians 3:20 KJV Now unto him that is able to do exceeding abundantly above all that we ask or think, according to the power that worketh in us.

2 Corinthians 9:8 KJV And God is able to make all grace abound toward you; that ye, always having all sufficiency in all things, may abound to every good work:

2 Corinthians 12:9 NIV But, he said to me, "My grace is sufficient for you, for my power is made perfect in weakness." Therefore, I will boast all the more gladly about my weaknesses, so that Christ's power may rest on me.

Declaration
Nothing is Impossible Because I Believe

I declare - I can do all things through Christ that strengthens me every day, every hour, and every minute. I am full of His power and glory! Greater is the Holy Spirit in me than he that is in the world. The Holy Spirit is my guide, He leads me and guides me into victory every day.

My steps are ordered. I can do all things because He is dwelling in me and working through me. He causes me to win! I am graced to do greater! I am marked to be greater! I am destined to achieve greater!

I will do great exploits for the Lord today because I know Him. Because I know Him, and He knows me, I am empowered to do exactly what I set out to achieve today. There is no impossible task, no goal too hard, no challenge insurmountable, no odds unbeatable and no enemy undefeatable with God.

With God, I am unstoppable, uncontainable, and undefeatable! He accomplishes exceeding, abundantly above all I can think or imagine according to the power that works in me. His grace is sufficient for me and abounding toward me continually. No situation can exhaust His grace on my life to win. He equips me daily to do the good work He already prepared for me.

He prepared the work for me and prepared me for the work. I am well able! I am strong enough! I am smart enough! I am enough! I can absolutely, without doubt, do all things through Christ. I am willing, prepared, equipped, empowered, and full of the anointing (the power to get results) of God.

My failure isn't final! My victory is secured! I decree and declare I can do all things through Christ, my Savior! Today, I can. Today, all things are possible for me!

Continue Your Declaration Here:

Day 4

"The enemy is speaking relentlessly and consistently over our children. Will you raise your voice to silence his?"

Hey Beautiful,

I once heard Dr. Rodrigues say, "Feelings are nothing more than demons." Oh man, was he right! Often, we make the tragic mistake of moving by our feelings. Feelings are from the devil! We give up on this declaring thing because we don't "feel" anything. Who said you would "feel" something? We get discouraged when we don't see manifestation instantaneously. Especially when it comes to our seed - our children. We want to see their behavior change immediately or see them start walking in purpose suddenly. We want our microwave perfect children right away. When we fail to see it in their behavior, hear it in their language, or feel it in our fleshly hearts, we get discouraged.

If you go back and read the beginning of Genesis in the Bible where we see the creative power of God at work, you won't read anything about His feelings. He spoke, and it happened! It wasn't based upon a feeling. The bible never said God got goose bumps or the hair on his arms stood up.

When Jesus cursed the fig tree for not producing, He simply cursed it and walked away. He didn't wait to feel something. He knew He had the authority to curse it and He operated in that authority. We must grow in faith to the degree that we speak and walk away.

Sometimes, with my children, I find that this can be the most difficult task. We want to feel that confirmation in our flesh. But God confirms His word in our hearts first (our spirit) and our external response is often a result of our personalities. He is doing it whether you feel it or not.

With our children, often, we want to give them to God and take them back when we feel God is moving too slow. We want to speak life over them but when we see them going down the wrong path, we want to insert our natural roadblocks. Many times, these roadblocks are threats, manipulation, and sarcasm thrust out by frustration and hopelessness, but God tells us to train them up in the way they should go, and they will not depart from it. He gives us the responsibility, authority, and ability to train them up and speak over them. He will do the rest. So, speak life and walk away with confidence knowing that what you curse must die and what you command to live must live.

Speak over your children; they will be saved. Speak over their future; the purposes of God will prevail. Speak over their body; they are the temple of the living God.

The enemy is speaking relentlessly and consistently over our children. Will you raise your voice to silence his? Speak and God will never neglect His part to perform!

Scripture Meditation

Deuteronomy 28:4 NIV The fruit of your womb will be blessed, and the crops of your land and the young of your livestock--the calves of your herds and the lambs of your flocks.

Genesis 22:18 NLT And through your descendants all the nations of the earth will be blessed--all because you have obeyed me.

Isaiah 44:3 NLT For I will pour out water to quench your thirst and to irrigate your parched fields. And I will pour out my Spirit on your descendants, and my blessing on your children.

Psalm 91:9-11 NLT If you make the LORD your refuge, if you make the Most High your shelter, no evil will conquer you; no plague will come near your home. For he will order his angels to protect you wherever you go.

Declaration
My Seed is Blessed

I declare as God has already decreed - the fruit of my womb is blessed. My seed is blessed and cannot be cursed. Every generational curse that is connected to my bloodline is destroyed and will not be carried, transferred, or delivered by the destroyer to my seed.

My child(ren) have power, love, and a sound mind. Confusion, chaos, negativity, and harmful thinking can't fester in their minds. They have the mind and character of Christ. Their environments are peaceful, and their heart is calmed.

I cancel every attack and assignment the enemy has on their life. I declare they are marked for God's use and His Kingdom purposes. His plan for them is good and will prevail! They will be used by God to advance His Kingdom on Earth. They will fulfill the assignment and destiny God has preordained for them. They are healthy, wealthy, and wise. I bind premature death, sickness, and disease. They will live long lives and see the goodness of our God.

I declare my children are full of witty ideas and million-dollar inventions. They are creators, builders, and inventors. They will create generational wealth and break curses of poverty in our bloodline. They are courageous leaders who are full of the power and presence of God.

My children have clean, pure hearts and it will manifest in their words and deeds. They are full of the perfect love of God and it spills out of them in all they do. They are full of compassion for people and that compassion drives them to help and assist others in need. They are strong in the Lord and the power of His might.

They have and operate in a spirit of excellence. They are examples of the awesomeness, intelligence, and creativity of God, excelling in every area! They are not ordinary but extraordinary gifts from God. The Holy Spirit is great in them and they are great because of Him.

I declare they will be brave, strong, and courageous as they face giants, challenges, and obstacles each day. They are gap fillers, prayer warriors, and mighty because they are clothed in the armor of God. The enemy can't touch them. I declare a blood covering over them. I break every attachment the enemy has tried to make. I close every door and I stand at every gate.

They are covered by the blood of the Lamb therefore they have protection, provision, and prosperity. The blood of Jesus shed for them is more than enough each and every day. All of their needs are supplied according to His riches in glory in Christ Jesus. They will not lack in any area - financially, emotionally, physically, or spiritually. Every need is met.

I declare they will not walk in the counsel of the ungodly nor take the path of sinners.

My sons will be priest, protectors, and providers. My daughters will be women of purpose, power, prayer, and praise. They will walk in integrity and Godly wisdom each and every day as their steps are ordered by God. I declare no weapon formed against them shall prosper!

I declare they are the head and not the tail, above and never beneath! I declare they are blessed beyond measure and the blessings and favor of God will overtake them all the days of their lives.

Continue Your Declaration Here:

Day 5

"The enemy would love for us to stay naive to the powerful love God extended to us through Jesus."

Hey Beautiful,

I found myself writing this to you with tears flowing! Tears of joy and gratefulness! Today, my heart is full of indescribable joy, as I reflect on the love of Jesus. What manner of love is this? The times in my life when I felt unworthy of love, the love of Jesus found me and healed me! When I was looking for love and acceptance in all the wrong places, His love snatched me out and ministered to the deepest parts of my soul.

In my darkest times, it was His love that lit up every dark space in me. His love became my source of strength and the center of my joy. There is so much power in the love that Christ has for us; it disarmed death and liberated us. This love that He has for us is so indescribable and incomprehensible.

How often do we love to boast about how much we love Jesus? That is wonderful and necessary. But, let me tell you my friend, one of the most powerful things you can learn to do or boast about is the love that Jesus has for you!

Now, *that* scares the enemy! The enemy would love for us to stay naive to the powerful love God extended to us through Jesus. He knows that our love is flawed and can fail. Yes, even the love we profess to have for our Father and His Son isn't perfect love. It's far from perfect! It doesn't always show up for Him and we don't always express it in our lifestyles and interactions with others.

But His love toward us is without flaws and worth bragging about. When we start shouting about how much God loves us with an unfailing, undying, undefeated love…my God! Whenever I say this declaration, the presence of God fills my heart and space. He completely embraces me with the weight of His love. Joy and gratefulness flow like a river when we reflect on His love!

We can learn how impactful it is to declare God's love for us through the life of David. David was described by God as a man after His own heart. He made it his mission to do the will of God. He was a worshipper, a lover of God. I learned something amazing from David; he often boasted, not about how much he loved God, but about how much God loved him.

In Psalm 51:1-12 – David repented to God and asked for mercy. It was not because he deserved it, but he said it was because of God's steadfast love for him. In Psalm 103, David proclaimed how great the Father's love is. In verse 8, he said that the love of God never fails. In verse 12, he asked - how great is God's love? Then David responded that His love is greater than the distance between heaven and earth.

David wasn't perfect; he was flawed and sinned, yet God loved him. God's love for David was based upon His faithfulness, not David's faithfulness. It's not something we earn, we just receive it! Because of His love, we are driven to do exploits in His name.

His love can't be explained. God's extravagant love for you and I, perplexes religious mindsets, destroys every barrier, climbs every mountain, and brings into captivity everything that seeks to separate us from Him. There is no limit to what He would do to go after one of His own.

Are you comprehending this?

Our Father has such an everlasting, excessive, possessive kind of love for us. Extravagant! The jealous kind! The love that leaves 99 behind to find one...You!

Our Father is completely reckless when it comes to the love He has for His children. We are His children - the very apple of His eye! He loves us without limits. Anytime the enemy tries to tell you something different, read this declaration and remind him and yourself of the immeasurable love of God for you!

Scripture Meditation

Romans 5:8 NIV But God demonstrates His own love for us in this: While we were still sinners, Christ died for us.

Romans 8:39 NLT No power in the sky above or in the earth below--indeed, nothing in all creation will ever be able to separate us from the love of God that is revealed in Christ Jesus our Lord.

1 John 4:10 NIV This is love: not that we loved God, but that He loved us and sent His Son as an atoning sacrifice for our sins.

John 3:16 NIV For God so loved the world that He gave His one and only Son, that whoever believes in Him shall not perish but have eternal life.

Declaration
I Receive the Extravagant Love of God

I am so loved by Jesus. I am passionately chased today by His love. He pursues me today with His grace and mercy. His compassion doesn't allow me to be consumed. I am enticed by His overwhelming, undying love for me. His love paid it all for me. His love refused to let me stay astray. He purchased me back with an everlasting love.

God loves me so much and expressed that unconditional love when He offered up His Son. What good things would He withhold from me? I am His daughter, the apple of His eye. Today, I receive God's redeeming love. Today, I receive God's forgiving love. Today, I receive God's healing love. Today, I receive God's curse breaking love.

His love empowers me! His love lifts me! His love heals me! His love draws me! His love keeps me! His love covers all my faults, destroys all my shame, and defeats all my guilt!

His Love is more powerful than my past. His love is more powerful than my mistakes. His love is more powerful than my doubts and fears. His love is more powerful than any hate spewed towards me.

His love is powerful and is filling every void in my heart. His love is invading every space of me, and I receive it. His love is flooding my heart and keeping my mind. His love is defeating depression and destroying demons for me. Oh, how He loves me!

I am loved! I declare I am a recipient of the powerful love of God. I didn't earn it, but today - I receive it! I don't always deserve it, but today - I receive it! I haven't always appreciated it, but today - I receive it!

I declare I am loved by God and a distributor of His love to people. I declare that absolutely nothing will separate me from the love of God.

Continue Your Declaration Here:

____

____

____

____

Day 6

"Change is inevitable when you are speaking the Word of God, applying the faith of God and releasing the power of God."

Hey Beautiful,

Can you believe that it's already day six? Don't you dare give up on speaking what God says concerning you! Something is shifting in the spirit realm and it's shifting in your favor. It will manifest in your life and you will begin to see the goodness of our Lord and Savior in the land of the living. I have learned that this declaring and confessing thing is work! But, it works! So, don't get weary or allow the devil to tell you that nothing is changing!

Change is inevitable when you are speaking the Word of God, applying the faith of God, and releasing the power of God. The funny thing is - confessing the Word of God more, doesn't make what we are confessing more true. The Word of God is pure and true, whether you confess it or not. The Word of God is true regardless of you speaking it or believing it. Proverbs 30:5 (KJV) tells us, " Every word of God is pure: he is a shield unto them that put their trust in him." So, what does confessing do?

See, this confessing thing is for you! It helps your doubt and unbelief. It renews your mind and thinking, so you can have the mind of Christ and speak the language of the Kingdom. Jesus already secured your victory... point, blank, and the period! I realize now, the more I say it, it helps me to walk in that victory! The more I say it, the more I believe it and can grab hold of it in this natural realm. It drowns my doubt and suffocates my fear!

Speaking it over and over activates my faith for it, whatever "it" is. Our faith is voice activated! That's why the scripture says faith comes by hearing *and* hearing *and* hearing - the Word of God. Hearing in that scripture (Romans 10:17), is a continual state. The more you speak it, the more you hear it, the more you believe it and the more you will be able to receive!

Think of a real good, juicy rumor you have heard that was pretty unimaginable at first. The more you heard it, the more people repeated it, the more weight that rumor received. The more you heard it, the more you believed it, right?! The more people tell you it can't work, or that you will never be anything, or you're just like your momma or daddy...the more you conform to those words.

Words are powerful, sticks and stones are not! Sometimes I can be right in the middle of a losing a battle, but the Word of God that declares "I am victorious in Christ" will rise up in me and immediately shut defeat down! I recommend that you memorize this declaration and give the enemy a black eye every single time he speaks defeat in any area of your life. Silence him by speaking up!

When he tries to discourage you in the present, remind him of his future! And whatever you do, speak victory over your life! The more you declare "victory belongs to Jesus and it belongs to me," the more you will believe it, receive it, and walk in the manifestation of it!

Let's walk this thing out! Are you ready to confess V.I.C.T.O.R.Y? I am!

Scripture Meditation:

Corinthians 15:57 NIV But thanks be to God! He gives us the victory through our Lord Jesus Christ!

Deuteronomy 20:4 ESV For the Lord your God is He who goes with you to fight for you against your enemies, to give you the victory.

Declaration
My Victory is Secure in Jesus

I am undeniably victorious in Christ! I have victory over death and sin, life challenges, sickness and disease, and victory on the battlefield of my mind! He secured my victory when He completed His assignment on the cross, rose, and defeated death, and snatch the keys from the enemy. Because He got up, I can live in victory every day!

Defeat isn't an option nor my portion. Jesus ascended and led captivity captive for me. I declare I will not be tied up, held down, shackled, chained, restrained, or trapped! I declare I am free to live victoriously.

Anything that could hold me, Jesus is holding! No weapon formed against my victory shall prosper. In all things, I am more than a conqueror through Christ who loves me! I am on the winning team and cannot lose. My steps are ordered by God and He leads me to victory. He will not allow my enemies to triumph over me. His compassion towards me will not allow me to be consumed.

The God of the angels' army's wars on my behalf. The Commander in Chief of Heaven is fighting my battles. The battle belongs to Him, but the victory belongs to me. I declare I am a child of the undefeated champion of the universe.

He humbles my enemies and makes them a footstool under my feet. He always causes me to triumph, to overcome, and subdue! He brings walls down for me and gives me access to my promise land. He disarms my enemy, so I can walk in destiny!

In Him I live, breath and have my being. In Him, there is no defeat! In Him, I am safe and secure! In Him, I am well able! In Him, my enemies are defeated! In Him, giants fall! In Him, my name is victory! In Him, I can do all things. In Him, I am more than a conquer!

I declare today I am in Him! Glory!

Continue Your Declaration Here:

Day 7

"You're anointed to speak healing, so open your mouth and speak life."

Hey Beautiful,

Let's just be real...sometimes it's just easier to believe God for other people. I know I struggled with releasing my faith for healing for myself but could boldly declare it for another person. Why is that? I have a few thoughts as to why this is a difficult task for us. I heard a preacher say, "if you think God made you sick, it will be hard to ask for healing." My God, how true is that?

First, we must understand the character of our loving God, whom by his own self-revelation in Exodus 15:26, is Jehovah Rapha. Jehovah Rapha is one of His seven covenant names. Jehovah Rapha means I am the Lord, I am your healer. Healing isn't just what He does, it is who He is. Rapha means to restore back to its useful state. God can restore you! I dare you to declare that full restoration is your portion!

Next, we must understand the reality of our righteousness. Our right standing with the Healer, is what qualifies us for healing. To be a recipient of healing and a distributor of it is based on our righteousness with the Father. If you don't know if you're in right standing with God, get right by accepting Jesus as your Lord and Savior! That is the only thing that makes you righteous. In other words - you can't earn healing, you just receive it when you receive salvation!

It's part of your salvation benefit package. Jesus, who knew no sin, became sin for us that we may become the righteousness of God in Christ. You may not feel like you deserve healing, but Jesus earned it for you. It was a part of the complete work He did on the cross. Healing is a benefit that we must not forget.

Psalm 103:1-4 KJV - Bless the Lord, O my soul: and all that is within me, bless His holy name. Bless the Lord, O my soul, and forget not all His benefits: Who forgiveth all thine iniquities; who healeth all thy diseases; Who redeemeth thy life from destruction; who crowneth thee with lovingkindness and tender mercies."

Healing is the children's bread. Verse 3 says, "GOD forgives all your sins and heals all your diseases." Don't believe God for the forgiveness of your sin, but not for your healing. He does both! He wants both for you. He has made both available to you. Jesus showed His authority and power to do both in Matthew 9:1-8, when He saved and healed.

Try Jesus! Apply Him and His blood to your sickness. Don't spend your entire life trying every medicine, remedy, doctor, specialist, therapist, and never try the Great Physician. There is a balm in Gilead; there is healing for every wound you have. This is a declaration you should declare every single day over your body even when you feel well. If you are experiencing symptoms, cast those symptoms down before they are able to manifest sickness by speaking the Word of God only.

Speak the solution, not the condition. You're anointed to speak healing, so open your mouth and speak life! You have the authority of the believer, the power of the Holy Spirit, and the Word of God! So, speak the Word of God concerning healing and watch the Healer show up! He isn't the God that used to heal or the God that is going to heal. He is - I am that I am - right now! He is your healer right now, right now, right now! He has already healed you!

Now, you speak it - so it can manifest. Faith is voice

activated, so activate your faith, release the Word of God, and receive your Healing today! I believe that as the word of God is released, your faith will be elevated, and healing will manifest.

Scripture Meditation

Psalm 107:20 KJV He sent his word, and healed them, and delivered them from their destructions.

Psalm 103:3 NLT He forgives all my sins and heals all my diseases.

Isaiah 53:4-5 KJV Surely he hath borne our griefs and carried our sorrows: yet we did esteem him stricken, smitten of God, and afflicted. But he was wounded for our transgressions, he was bruised for our iniquities: the chastisement of our peace was upon him; and with his stripes we are healed.

Acts 10:38 KJV God anointed Jesus of Nazareth with the Holy Ghost and with power: who went about doing good and healing all that were oppressed of the devil."

Exodus 15:26 ESV If you will diligently listen to the voice of the LORD your God, and do that which is right in his eyes, and give ear to his commandments and keep all his statutes, I will put none of the diseases on you that I put on the Egyptians, for I am the LORD, your healer.

Matthew 14:14 KJV And Jesus went forth, and saw a great multitude, and was moved with compassion toward them, and he healed their sick.

Matthew 8:16 -17 KJV he cast out the spirits with his word, and healed all that were sick: That it might be fulfilled which was spoken by Esaias the prophet, saying, Himself took our infirmities, and bare our sicknesses.

Declaration
Divine Healing Belongs to Me

I declare that divine health is my portion. I declare that I am a righteous daughter, through Christ, of Jehovah Rapha! He is my healer. He does all things well. He makes all things new. He restores every part of me back to its useful and intended state.

I am forgiven of my sins and I am healed! My body is the temple of God and I send the Holy Spirit on assignment to search the temple and expose and evict everything that is harmful to the temple. It must leave now in the name of Jesus.

The same spirit that raised Jesus from the dead is dwelling in me. Quicken my body! My healing was secured over 2,000 years again and no devil can rob me of what belongs to me. Jesus carried my pain, put on my diseases, and by His stripes I am healed.

I declare that I am healed from every curse of the law. Christ purchased my freedom from the chains of sickness and gave me divine health. I declare nothing is more powerful than the blood shed on my behalf. Jesus heals every manner of sickness and disease; nothing is outside of the scope of his healing power!

He gives sight to the blind and heals the lame! He heals lepers! He heals every issue of blood! He restores strength, makes the dumb to speak, and He raises the dead. There is nothing, absolutely nothing, too hard for my God.

I am healed because of His compassion. I am healed because

it brings the Father glory. I am healed because that's my portion. I am healed because the atonement includes healing for my body. I am healed because He said I was!

I shall live and not die! Goodness and mercy shall follow me! I am walking in His healing grace! No weapon formed against my body shall be able to prosper! The name of Jesus is exalted above all other names and all sickness must bow to His name.

So, I speak the name of Jesus over my body! I speak the name of Jesus over every organ, joint, cell, all tissue and muscle, and my mind! You must bow and come into alignment with the Word of God. All sickness, all disease, and every attack on my health must bow NOW! Bow, bow, bow - to the name of Jesus Christ the Messiah! Bow to the Savior of the world - Jesus!

Continue Your Declaration Here:

____

____

____

____

____

____

____

____

____

____

____

____

____

Day 8

"We can't be lazy and possess all God has made available for you and I."

Hey Beautiful,

I'm learning that you can't be lazy and live the abundant life that God has made available. I recently wrote a short article for a magazine. In it, I spoke about positional truth and how many times we don't get every benefit that comes with our salvation due to lack of knowledge or laziness.

I had a moment of transparency and shared my own personal struggle with the demon called laziness. I had been working for this company for eight years. I attended school working on various degrees, while working for this amazing company. I didn't know that tuition reimbursement was a part of my benefit package because no one told me. I had been completely robbed.

The first perpetrator was the lack of knowledge, which I blamed on the person who hired me. She shared with me most of my benefits but neglected to tell me about the tuition reimbursement program. Years later, I became aware and gained knowledge of this available benefit then the robber became myself and good old faithful laziness. I didn't want to take the time and put in the work and apply for the available benefit.

Often, as Christians, there are so many benefits available to us that we never grab hold of. We don't because of our insufficient knowledge of the benefit package or laziness to do the work to enjoy the benefits. Jesus did the hard work or heavy lifting. You simply have to speak it, believe it, and receive it. If you think about it...the work is minute in comparison to what you will receive?

We can't be lazy and possess all that God has made available for you and I. Lack, insufficiency, mediocracy, barely making it, trying to make ends meet - doesn't have to be your portion. We serve the God of more than enough! He is the God of the overflow, the sufficient supplier, the one with unlimited access!

I'm trying to tell you, it all belongs to Him! The earth is the Lord's and the fullness thereof. We serve the King of Kings and Lord of Lords, who has adopted us and made us joint heirs! We are His children! Wow! Look at the provision He has made not just for your soul, but for your life! He is a good, good Father!

Scripture Meditation

Psalm 23:5 KJV Thou preparest a table before me in the presence of mine enemies: thou anointest my head with oil; my cup runneth over.

Psalm 103:2 KJV Bless the LORD, O my soul, and forget not all his benefits.

Philippians 4:19 KJV But my God shall supply all your need according to his riches in glory by Christ Jesus.

2 Corinthians 9:8 KJV And God is able to make all grace abound toward you; that ye, always having all sufficiency in all things, may abound to every good work.

1 Chronicles 29:12 ESV Both riches and honor come from You, and You rule over all, and in Your hand is power and might; and it lies in Your hand to make great and to strengthen everyone.

2 Peter 1:3 NIV His divine power has given us everything we need for a godly life through our knowledge of him who called us by his own glory and goodness.

Matthew 6:31-33 NASB Do not worry then, saying, 'What will we eat?' or 'What will we drink?' or 'What will we wear for clothing?' For the Gentiles eagerly seek all these things; for your heavenly Father knows that you need all these things. But seek first His kingdom and His righteousness, and all these things will be added to you.

Declaration
My Cup Runneth Over

I am a daughter of the Lord of the overflow. He is the God of abundance! He is the God of provision and He is my God! He is the God of supernatural increase and He is my God! He causes all grace to abound toward me and I have sufficiency in all things. My cup runs over daily because of all of His riches in glory.

I am blessed in the city, in the fields, when I come and when I go. I am blessed and cannot be cursed! His blessings are chasing me down and overtaking me today. He prepares a table for me in the presence of my enemies. I am a recipient of the abundant provision of God. Every good and perfect thing comes from him. I receive them all.

He goes before me and prepares for me, everything I need. I am a sower therefore I reap the blessings of the Lord. He continues to give me seed to sow and multiples my harvest. I plant on good ground and my harvest is returning pressed down, shaken together, and running over. I declare my harvest is plenty and I am calling it forth. Come forth from the North, South, East, and West!

I will not worry about anything, but I will release my faith to receive the provisions God has already made available to me. I seek His Kingdom first and He adds all other things to me.

I declare God is El Shaddai in my life and I always have more than enough. God provides all I need for life and Godliness.

He supplies my spiritual, physical, and emotional needs and I lack nothing. I declare I lack nothing at all because He is my God. He is God, my great supplier. God, my provider! God, my source! God, my sustainer! God, my multiplier! God, my everything!

Continue Your Declaration Here:

Day 9

"Declare, "I am powerful," until you feel like throwing a rock at every giant in your life!"

Hey Beautiful,

Silence is no longer an option! Oh, daughter of Zion, put on your strength and declare what thus says the Lord. Take up this weapon, the sword of the Spirit, and confess the Word of God over your life. The Word of God is living, active and sharper than any double-edged sword when it is released from your mouth. Release, woman of God!

War with your prayers, with your declarations, and with your confessions! Fight! War with your words. Stop using your words to dismantle your destiny and use them to build, to birth, to produce, to speak life, and to silence the enemy. Open your mouth and speak Zion!

His Word is so powerful and effective. You don't have to perform the Word of God, He will perform His own Word over your life. He is watching and waiting to perform it. You just have to speak it, believe it, and receive it. It was by the Word of the Lord that the heavens were made, and it will be by your words that heaven will bombard earth.

You can bring heaven right down into your situation. Hell will no longer be your place of residency when you begin to speak using heavenly language, activating Kingdom principles, and releasing Kingdom faith. Heaven will come! Kingdom, come!

Faith talk is the language that brings the Kingdom down! We declare, thine Kingdom come - NOW. God has prepared some stuff for you and I want you to receive it NOW - here on Earth. It is no longer an option for you to sit silently on the sidelines of your life, watching in a hopeless state.

Why are you allowing the enemy to win a game that is yours for the taking? You are powerful my friend, the MVP of your life. So, suit up - it's your turn! Put on the whole armor of God and take your stance! God is mighty in battle and so are you! The Kingdom of God suffers violent attack, but the violent take it by force! This is no job for the passive, pretty people! This is an assignment for the violent warriors.

Stop allowing the enemy to wreak havoc in your life. Satan is a dangerous enemy armed with trickery, but you are a worthy opponent! You can take him down! You can take control and put him to flight. Put him where he belongs - under your feet, not on your back. He is a completely defeated foe!

Declare that he is defeated in your marriage! Declare that he is defeated in your ministry! Declare that he is defeated in your finances! Declare that he is defeated in your mind! Declare that you are full of power, glory, authority, and that heaven responds to you! Angelic armies are dispatched at your request! The Holy Spirit responds when you speak! You are powerful! Declare, "I am powerful" until you feel like throwing a rock at every giant in your life!

You are anointed to speak to your mountains! You are anointed to throw a rock that kills your enemy! You are anointed to destroy yokes! You are anointed to silence the enemy! You are anointed to break generational curses! You are anointed!

How will you respond to the power that has been released to you?

If God is for you, who can be against you? Who can silence you? Who can stop you? Who? Only *you,* my friend! So, get out of your own way. Put on strength and use the power and authority you have been given to overcome everything! You are anointed, my friend.

Do you know what the anointing has the ability to do? You couldn't possibly know and *not* release it through the power of your declarations. See, we aren't just saying stuff - we are *ANOINTED* to do this! And because we are anointed, we get results! So, speak your declaration today like you know that you are anointed to do so!

Scripture Meditation

Romans 8:37 NKJV Yet in all these things we are more than conquerors through Him who loved us.

Revelation 12:11 KJV And they overcame him by the blood of the Lamb, and by the word of their testimony; and they loved not their lives unto the death.

Romans 8:31 KJV What shall we then say to these things? If God be for us, who can be against us?

1 Peter 5:8 KJV Be sober, be vigilant; because your adversary the devil, as a roaring lion, walketh about, seeking whom he may devour.

Colossians 2:14-15 KJV Blotting out the handwriting of ordinances that was against us, which was contrary to us, and took it out of the way, nailing it to his cross; And having spoiled principalities and powers, he made a shew of them openly, triumphing over them in it.

Declaration
I Am Powerfully Anointed!

I am a powerful warrior and overcomer in Christ! I slay giants and conquer impossible things because of the greater One in me! Yes, in all things and situations, I am more than a conquer. I am the head and not the tail, above and not beneath.

I am a soldier in the Lord's army, armed and dangerous to

the kingdom of darkness. I declare that I am strong in the Lord and the power of His might. My loins are girded about with truth. I have on the breastplate of righteousness. My feet are shod with the preparation of the gospel. I have the shield of faith and the helmet of salvation. I am fully armed with the sword of the Spirit!

Today, I put out every fiery dart he is aiming at me and those connected to me. I declare that I will not be blind to the enemy's tactics, schemes, plots, or plans. He is exposed, and I am victorious. I declare I am sober, vigilant, and violent for the Kingdom of God. I declare I am an imitator of God and He is mighty and strong in battle. No weapon formed against me shall be able to prosper. God exposes my enemies; I will not be confused or unclear about who my enemy is.

My wrestle is not with flesh and blood, but against spiritual forces of wickedness in the heavenly places. My battle is spiritual, and I am armed, equipped, and anointed to win. I declare, no matter what the enemy throws at me today, (persecution, tribulation, sickness, distress, disappointment, pain, lack) I will overwhelmingly conquer it all!

He always causes me to triumph, to rise, to subdue, to come forth, and to come out! I am victorious because I have full access to the Commander-in-Chief of the Lord's army. I am victorious because I live in the presence of God. I am victorious because He loves me. Nothing will be able to separate me from God or His love for me.

I declare the love of God is what makes me a conqueror, and that is why I can't be consumed by evil. I am loved by God! He is my fortress, my strong tower, my protection, and shield! Whom shall I fear? I declare that He is for me and it doesn't matter what or who is against me.

He makes my high places low and gives me access to my promise land. He is my keeper and ever-present help in my time of trouble. I declare I am powerful because I am loved by God. I am anointed because I am a child of God. I am covered because I am in the Kingdom of God. Nothing, by any means, shall be able to harm me. I have the power and authority today to tread on snakes and scorpions.

Today, I command every enemy to submit to the authority I have been given and to stay under my feet all day long. You will not operate illegally in my life. God reigns in my life and you will not! I have an advantage. The anointing on my life releases protection, provision, unlocks doors, manifest healing, gives me wisdom, revelation, and knowledge. I declare I have access because of the anointing. I have favor because of the anointing.

Today, I will get results in every area of my life because of the anointing. I am super productive and effective because of the anointing. I declare that oil flows today and meets every one of my needs. I declare the anointing is cancelling debt on my behalf. I am more than a conqueror because I am anointed. And I declare that this anointing doesn't just bless others, but today - it blesses me!

I am anointed to bless myself, and I command the blessing of the Lord to overtake me! I am anointed to break the yoke, and I command every yoke to be destroyed now! I am anointed to heal the sick, and I command all sickness to bow to the name of Jesus! I am anointed for wealth, and I call it forth now!

I am anointed!

Continue Your Declaration Here:

____

____

____

____

Day 10

"When you arise - our mighty God, full of might and power, will arise and disappoint your enemies. Arise! Arise! Arise!"

Hey Beautiful,

What is holding you back today? Do you believe that God wants you to L.I.V.E (Live in Victory Everyday)? Do you believe that the Father wants you healthy - physically, mentally, and emotionally? Many times, we don't see results because we lack consistency in our walk with him. We are hot one day and cold another. Up, on high highs, then as low as we can go. The bible calls that double-minded and unstable and it disqualifies us from experiencing our abundant life. God wants you stable, planted, firm on the foundation of His Word, and rooted and grounded in this walk. He wants you standing on His promises and unwavering in your faith.

We often hear that consistency gets results, yet we lack the power, will, and drive to be consistent. God doesn't just want us to have fruit, but to remain in it and that takes consistency. The same thing you did to get the fruit, is the same thing you must do to remain fruitful. You have to continue in prayer, continue in worship, continue dwelling in the secret place of the Most High God, continue in fasting and other spiritual disciplines. Continue, because consistency will block the enemy from coming in!

Discipline will keep you fruitful and faithful. We have to be fruitful in the Kingdom and have enough fruit, that others who are struggling can pick from our tree! Where is your fruit? Your fruit stabilizes you! We can't be emotionally and mentally unstable and operate in Kingdom principles.

God didn't create our bodies to deal with instability, stress, depression, anxiety, fear, chaos, confusion, or disease. We aren't supposed to be hopeless and defeated. That's why He commands us in 1 Peter 5:7 to "cast all our anxiety on Him because He cares for us." The scripture goes on to say, "be sober minded because the devil "is like" a roaring lion seeking whom he may devour." But our God is the roaring lion of Judah and He will devour the enemy who is trying to steal our peace! The mind regulator will release His perfect peace over our mind daily when we remain in Him! But you can't remain in Him, unstable!

You can't be sober minded and double minded at the same time! No ma'am! But you can choose! You can choose to cast your cares on Him daily and He will exchange it with His peace that surpasses all understanding. It is His peace that will guard your heart, according to Philippian 4:7. You will stand firm, when you come boldly to the throne with confidence and cast your cares on the One who can carry them. He says take my yoke upon you, it is easy, and my burden is light. Give Him what you can't bear, and He will give you what you can! In Matthew 11:28, He tells you that you can come to Him weary and burdened, and He will give you rest. You can't experience sufficient rest, when there is a battle in your mind.

You must understand that the enemy wants you sick - emotionally and mentally, because you are at your weakest state and unable to fight spiritually. But, when you are weak, our Father is strong! Allow Him to arise in you and silence the voices in your mind. How do you allow Him to arise? You arise!

When you arise - our mighty God, full of power and might, will arise and disappoint your enemies. Arise! Arise! Arise! You have to take some action! You are waiting on Him to move and He is waiting on you to catch up!

I call forth that sleeping warrior in you that has been silent long enough. Arise sleeping beauty! Arise and start confessing over your mind. Arise and start confessing over your emotions! Arise and start confessing over those negative thoughts! Arise and start confessing over those suicidal moments! Arise and start confessing over that depression!

Arise! Arise and speak life! Arise and speak victory! Arise and speak the joy of the Lord over yourself! Arise and speak the peace of the Lord over your mind! Come on beautiful! You are a powerful warrior and I command that fighter in you to arise and come forth in the name of Jesus! Soldier wake up, get up, and suit up! Take your position and get ready to fight!

Now, let's speak from that risen state! Depression, anxiety, and fear are all spirits and those spirits will respond to the Word of God! You're not hopeless or helpless. You are whole in Him who died for you! Nothing can remain broken, damaged, or lacking in you. Healing is manifesting as you declare today. The joy of the Lord strengthens you - now, so that you can release this declaration into your atmosphere and watch your atmosphere shift!

Scripture Meditation:

Matthew 11:28 NIV Come to me, all you who are weary and burdened, and I will give you rest.

1 Peter 5:7-8 KJV Casting all your care upon him; for he careth for you. Be sober, be vigilant; because your adversary the devil, as a roaring lion, walketh about, seeking whom he may devour.

Philippians 4:6-7 KJV Be careful for nothing; but in every thing by prayer and supplication with thanksgiving let your requests be made known unto God. And the peace of God, which passeth all understanding, shall keep your hearts and minds through Christ Jesus.

2 Corinthians 10:5 KJV Casting down imaginations, and every high thing that exalteth itself against the knowledge of God and bringing into captivity every thought to the obedience of Christ.

Proverbs 12:25 NKJV Anxiety in the heart of man causes depression, but a good word makes it glad.

James 1:6-8 KJV But let him ask in faith, nothing wavering. For he that wavers is like a wave of the sea driven with the wind and tossed. For let not that man think that he shall receive any thing of the Lord. A double minded man is unstable in all his ways.

John 8:36 NIV So if the Son sets you free, you will be free indeed.

Isaiah 61:3 KJV To appoint unto them that mourn in Zion, to give unto them beauty for ashes, the oil of joy for mourning, the garment of praise for the spirit of heaviness; that they might be called trees of righteousness, the planting of the LORD, that he might be glorified.

Matthew 11:29-30 KJV Take my yoke upon you and learn of me; for I am meek and lowly in heart: and ye shall find rest unto your souls. For my yoke is easy, and my burden is light.

Psalm 37:23-24 KJV The steps of a good man are ordered by the LORD: and he delighteth in his way. Though he fall, he shall not be utterly cast down: for the LORD upholdeth him with his hand.

Declaration
I am Whole in Him

I declare that I will be physically, emotionally, and mentally healthy because the name of Jesus still has power. At His name, everything that can be named must bow. I declare that the chain breaker is breaking every chain off my mind and body. I will not live bound, chained, or wrapped up. I command all grave clothes, all chains, and bondage to fall off me now. I am the property of God; I have been redeemed. I declare I am walking in total deliverance and freedom.

Today, I win on the battlefield of my mind because I cast the enemy out! I cast down imagination and every high thing that exalts itself against the knowledge of God. Right now, I bring every thought into captivity, to the obedience of Christ. I declare I am firm and stable, with a sound mind and unwavering faith. I will not be tossed, shaken, overwhelmed or uprooted.

The fire of the Lord is burning everything around me that comes to steal, kill, and destroy my peace. I command heaviness to lift as I put on the garment of praise today. I declare that depression, anxiety, turmoil, defeat, rage, and fear must lift off me. The lifter is here! The lifter is in me! I will not be agitated, aggravated, irritated, distracted, or frustrated.

Peace is my portion! Peace belongs to me! I speak the peace of God over myself today. I declare that every atmosphere I step into will be peaceful. I bind all peace disturbers, joy killers, serenity stealers, and spiritual agitators. You can't have my tranquility.

I declare that I will not operate in fear, depression, double-mindedness, anxiety, or confusion. For the Lord has given me peace, love, and a sound-mind. Therefore, my mind is sound!

My emotions are regulated! My flesh is crucified! I am walking in the spirit, with the fruit of the spirit operating in me. Out of my belly is flowing rivers of living water.

The Spirit of God is arising in me now and exposing and confusing my enemy! My helper is here! The sun shall not smite me by day nor the moon by night. He is preserving my soul and keeping me from evil. He will not allow my foot to be moved. He will not allow my enemy to triumph over me! I am dwelling in the secret place of the Most - High God and abiding under his shadow. He is my refuge, fortress, and ever-present help in my time of trouble!

I declare that I will not fear, for He is with me. I am not alone. I am protected. He is my shield and my buckler. He cares greatly for me. His angels have charge over me. He is keeping me.

I declare I will not lose my mind, my sanity, or my life. With long life, He will satisfy me.

I declare depression must go! I declare anxiety must depart! I declare fear has expired! I declare confusion is evicted! I declare low self-esteem is being driven out by Word and Spirit of the living God.

I declare I am free, healed, and whole! No longer bound! Every curse is broken off my life. I declare, no more chains! No more bondage! No more sleepless nights! No more turmoil! No more anxiety! No more fear! No longer broken! I am totally free in the name of Jesus!

Continue Your Declaration Here:

____

____

____

Day 11

"Our words are mere words until they are thrust out by the very Spirit of the living God."

Hey Beautiful,

So, this is an interesting way to start this letter, but for lack of a better segway - Do you know Him? Does He lead you? Can you feel His empowerment? His power? Are your words saturated in His anointing?

Our words are mere words until they are thrust out by the very Spirit of the living God. You may start off speaking these declarations out of your own mouth, in your own might, but you will know the minute it switches to the voice of the Holy Spirit. Something shifts! There is a level of boldness that comes to stand in authority and declare the Word of God over your situation when you yield your voice to the Holy Spirit.

The Holy Spirit releases to us what to declare because He knows the Word of God and the heart of the Father. He elevates our confessions, He enlarges our capacity to confess, and He empowers our declarations. He anoints us for our mission. We read in scripture that after Jesus was baptized at the Jordan, He (the Holy Spirit) descended like a dove and rested on Jesus right before He began His mission of healing mankind and redeeming us. He empowered Him to carry out the mission.

We need Him for our mission of declaring and confessing. He gives us confidence and perseverance to speak those invisible things until they manifest. He strengthens us when we want to give up. He launches our declarations to the heavenly realms. He imparts a burden for others and we are able to pray and declare for people that we don't even know.

You will go from declaring for yourself to speaking over an entire nation when the boldness, knowledge, and wisdom of the Holy Spirit is birthed in you and ignites your fire. Often, I remind myself how much I need His igniting.

God accomplishes His purpose in us through the power of the Holy Spirit. The Holy Spirit, who was an agent in creation, hovering over the face of waters and breathing on the very words of God, lives in you. We need Him to breath on our words today! Oh, how we need His partnership in declaring the things of the Kingdom.

He is our comforter or counselor which translates from the Greek word parakletos. This word describes one called to the side of another. The Holy Spirit is the one who walks right beside our spirit man. The Paraclete, the great Counselor is God the Holy Spirit. He is the third Person of the Trinity and lives in every believer. We need Him, and He is available to every believer. Even if you don't feel Him, He is there. I had to learn to speak and believe the Holy Spirit was in me, before I ever "felt" him. Because He is in us, we are equipped and empowered to speak life!

The Holy Spirit empowers us to do great things for the Kingdom of God. Without Him, your declaration lacks power. Without power, you will not produce in the Spirit! In Acts 1:8, Jesus lets us know that we shall receive power when the Spirit comes upon us. We need the Holy Spirit inside of us, to come upon us when we speak the Word of God and when we receive it! He gives revelation and illumination. He adds the acceleration to what we are declaring! He is the gas! He is the power source, the powerhouse of the Godhead! We can't be effective without Him.

My prayer is that if you have been speaking these

declarations without the power of the Holy Spirit, you will start over! I couldn't write and deposit this devotional into your life without Him and you can't receive the manifestation of it without Him. We simply can't do it without Him, which is why the helper was sent. The Father and the Son knew we couldn't do it alone. When we needed a Savior, God wrapped Himself in flesh, stepped out of eternity into our reality, we beheld Him! When He ascended, we were in need of a teacher, a guide, a comforter, and power to do greater works so He sent the Holy Spirit that came like a mighty rushing wind and filled our temples. Our temples became His dwelling place.

The Holy Spirit is a sweet gift to every believer that must be received. You can have a gift and never open it! As a matter of fact, many Christian are walking around powerless because they haven't opened the gift of the Holy Spirit. Jesus, being full of the Holy Spirit, was led by the Holy Spirit, even into the wilderness. How much more do we need the Holy Spirit to lead us, sustain us, strengthen us, and give us the Word of God to use against the enemy of God?

Pray this prayer with me: "Holy Spirit, forgive me for not fully receiving you, not welcoming you, and not communing with you. I ask and give you permission to come upon me that I may declare with power, the word of the Lord. Bring illumination and fire! Bring fire and wind! Bring demonstration like only You can do!

I will no longer attempt to operate, speak, pray or even move without You. Consume me! Ignite me! Empower me! Speak to me and through me! Holy Spirit, have Your way in me! I submit to Your leading! Fill me with the evidence of speaking in other tongues. Spirit, give me utterance! Spirit of the living God, put fire on my declarations! Spirit of the living God, flow like a river in me! Spirit of the living God, erupt in me!"

I'm believing God, that the same Spirit, the same wind, the

same fire and power that I feel while releasing this to you, will rest on you - now. You will never be able to operate the same! Fire! Fresh Fire! Fresh oil! Fresh! Wind blow - now!! Just receive! Sit in His presence and receive! He wants to pour. He desires to fill you up.

Do you have time to receive? Do you want to receive? Are you hungry for Him? God, release a new hunger to us that can only be satisfied in Your presence. He promises that when we hunger and thirst after Him, He will fill us. He won't leave you hungry. He won't leave you dry. He won't leave you barren. He won't leave you lacking. He won't leave you unfulfilled. He will fill you, today. He will fill us daily! We need that infilling and refilling daily! We will overflow! We will live in the overflow, operate in the overflow, others will drink from our overflow!

Speak this declaration with boldness until the power of the Holy Spirit erupts in you, like a volcano! Unleash the Holy Spirit by opening your mouth and declaring the Word of the Lord!

Scripture Meditation:

John 14:15-17 NIV If you love me, keep my commands. And I will ask the Father, and he will give you another advocate to help you and be with you forever - the Spirit of truth. The world cannot accept him, because it neither sees him nor knows him. But you know him, for he lives with you and will be [c] in you.

John 16:8 NIV When he comes, he will prove the world to be in the wrong about sin and righteousness and judgment.

Genesis 1:2 ESV The earth was without form and void, and darkness was over the face of the deep. And the Spirit of God was hovering over the face of the waters.

Galatian 5:16-18 (ESV) So I say, walk by the Spirit, and you will not gratify the desires of the flesh. For the flesh craves what is contrary to the Spirit, and the Spirit what is contrary to the flesh. They are opposed to one another, so that you do not do what you want. But if you are led by the Spirit, you are not under the Law.

John 14:16 ESV And I will ask the Father, and he will give you another helper, to be with you forever.

John 16:7 ESV Nevertheless, I tell you the truth: it is to your advantage that I go away, for if I do not go away, the Helper will not come to you. But if I go, I will send him to you.

Galatians 5:25 NLT Since we are living by the Spirit, let us follow the Spirit's leading in every part of our lives.

Declaration
I am Empowered by the Holy Spirit

I receive the baptism of the Holy Spirit, my gift from God! I declare I am empowered by the Spirit of the living God. Today, I receive a fresh impartation and infilling of Him. Like a mighty rushing wind, come Holy Spirit, rest upon me. Dwell in me! Rise up in me! Quicken me!

Stir me! Fill me! Ignite my fire! I declare I am open to receive from you today. I declare I am open to be used by You today. I am a carrier of the Glory of God. His Spirit resides in me.

Rivers of living water flow out of me. I am full of the Spirit of God and I operate under the influence of the Holy Spirit. I am empowered by Him to witness, love, and serve. I declare I will not grieve You, quench, nor resist you today.

I declare the Holy Spirit is my teacher, my guide, my helper, my counselor, my leader, and my power source. I declare my body is the temple of God and the dwelling place of the Holy

Spirit. I give Him access to every area of my temple. I give Him permission to search my temple and evict any and everything that is contrary to or in conflict with the Word of God.

Purify me, Holy Spirit! Purge me! Regenerate my heart and sanctify me! Consume me, Holy Spirit! Immerse me, Holy Spirit and baptize me with fire! Dominate my flesh! Activate my faith! Release Your power! Overwhelm me with Your presence!

I declare more of You and less of me. I declare that because You have been poured out upon me, Holy Spirit, I shall prophesy, dream dreams, see visions, and demonstrate power!

Counselor, be my guide. Comforter, heal my hurt! Helper, help me today! Advocate, intercede through me! Give me utterance. Spirit of truth, give me new revelation and insight today. Spirit of wisdom and understanding, bring enlightenment today! Holy Spirit, take complete control. Order my steps!

I declare I will walk in the Spirit and operate in the fruit of the Spirit. I declare I am full of the Holy Spirit! I yield completely to you today Holy Spirit!

Continue Your Declaration Here:

Day 12

"When God speaks to us about our future, it is always contrary and conflicting to what is currently in front of us."

Hey Beautiful,

Let's be real! One of the most difficult things to do is to change your language when your vision remains the same. But, it can be done, and you *are* doing it! You can change what you say, even when what you see with your natural eyes hasn't changed...YET!

We live in a world where negative things are blasted on social media feeds, news outlets, and are often the hot topic of discussion in social settings and even the workplace. How do you consistently see and hear all the devastation in our world, homes, and personal situations and continue to speak on a higher level? Well, it takes some supernatural determination, discipline, and strength.

I pray that determination, discipline, and the supernatural strength of God is released to you today! Strength and drive to speak those things you want to see and not what you currently see. The enemy would love for you to focus more on what it looks like and less on what it could look like. If he can get and keep you discouraged by the conditions around you, he will silence your declarations and as a result, detour or delay the manifestations. But don't allow him to win! Not today!

It doesn't matter how hopeless and helpless you feel your situation is, God still has a plan for your life! He is still speaking that plan over you. He is yet thinking good thoughts toward you. His thoughts of you are good, even if someone's words against you are bad! His thoughts are good, even if your situation is bad!

Aren't you so glad that Jeremiah 29:11 says, I know the thoughts I THINK toward you, not *thought* toward you. Yes, our Father is still thinking about you. He still has you and I on His mind. He hasn't forgotten about you. I love the way the message bible gives us Jeremiah 29:11. It reads in verses10-11, "this is God's Word on the Subject: "As soon as Babylon's seventy years are up and not a day before, I'll show up and take care of you as I promised and bring you back home. I know what I am doing. I have it all planned out-plans to take care of you, not abandon you, plans to give you the future you hope for." Our God knows what He is doing; He has it ALL planned out. Therefore, you must remain confident of this very thing, that He that has begun a good work in you, will perfect it!

You can't be moved by your current situation; your NOW isn't your Next! Your NOW isn't final! God has a future for you. In that text, future is translated often as "an expected end" or "a ground of hope." It is noteworthy that God spoke about this hope to the children of Israel while they were in Captivity in Babylon. Gods speaks life when we are in dire situations.

He is speaking great and marvelous things concerning you right now, regardless of what you are facing. You must in turn, speak life when all odds are stacked against you and the words you are speaking are completely contrary to what you are seeing.

When God speaks about the future, it is always contrary and conflicting to what is in front of us. David didn't look like a King! Esther didn't look like a Queen! That is what this faith walk is all about. It is conflict between our now and our next, between our flesh and our spirit, our present and our future, our situation, and our purpose.

Be encouraged today, my friend, God is still thinking about you and speaking what He already spoke about you before the foundation of the world. And those thoughts and words trump what others have said, are saying, and will say concerning you. When people have given up on you and thrown their hands up, God extends His hands! He pleads - come close daughter, I have a good plan for your life and it is one of hope and a future.

He gently reminds you that it doesn't matter what has tainted your past, it didn't disqualify you for His plan for your future! He is the God who always goes before you and prepares a place for you and I. He told the disciples that He was going before them to prepare a place for them. That is how our Father operates. He goes before you and makes room for you, opens doors for you, and prepares a table for you in the presence of your enemies. He has a prepared place, a prepared destiny, a prepared purpose for your life! Your past only processed you. It prepared you for what He has prepared for you.

I love the process in which a pearl is produced. How? I am so glad you asked! It is pretty amazing! When an oyster gets a small grain of sand in its shell, it becomes irritated and begins to attempt to force the sand out. If unsuccessful it grows more and more frustrated! Out of aggravation and irritation, it begins to coat the pearl over and over and over, until the result is a very valuable gem that we spend our good coins for! What am I saying to you?

All of your past frustrations, irritations, aggravations, have produced something so valuable that this world will spend good coins for! They need your book, your message, your business, and they will pay top dollar for it because it is valuable. God didn't need sugar and spice and everything nice to make you good to serve to this dying world, He needed that ugly stuff. He needed that stuff you work so hard to bury and sweep under the rug. That stuff you are still carrying shame and condemnation over. The embarrassing, don't want to think about, hard to talk about, tough stuff.

Understand this, love - your past may not be pretty, but you are powerful because of it! And in Christ, you yet have a hope and a future. That's a good place to give him a YET praise. I messed up, YET God kept me! I didn't have a plan, YET God had a purpose! I didn't cross every T, YET he called me!

Let's declare how bright our future is and send doubt, shame, and defeat fleeing.

Scripture Meditation

Jeremiah 29:11 NIV For I know the plans I have for you," declares the LORD, "plans to prosper you and not to harm you, plans to give you hope and a future.

Proverbs 23:18 ESV Surely there is a future, and your hope will not be cut off.

Proverbs 19:21 NIV Many are the plans in a person's heart, but it is the LORD's purpose that prevails.

Psalm 139:16-17 NKJV Your eyes saw my substance, being yet unformed. And in Your book, they all were written, the days fashioned for me, when as yet there were none of them. How precious also are Your thoughts to me, O God! How great is the sum of them!

Matthew 10:29-31 NET Aren't two sparrows sold for a penny? Yet not one of them falls to the ground apart from your Father's will. Even all the hairs on your head are numbered.

Psalm 40:5 KJV Many, O Lord my God, are Your wonderful works which You have done; and Your thoughts toward us cannot be counted. If I would declare and speak of them, they are more than can be numbered.

Daniel 11:32b KJV ... but the people that do know their God shall be strong and do exploits.

Declaration
God's Thoughts and Plans for Me Are Good

God is thinking precious thoughts concerning me today. His thoughts for me can't be numbered. They are more than the stars in the sky and the sand on the beach. I am always on the mind of God.

The creator of the universe is thinking of me right now. His thoughts of me are good and not evil. His thoughts of me are thoughts of adoration and not condemnation. God is declaring a hope and a future over me, even when people are speaking ill of me. He has a divine purpose and plan for my life. I am significant to God.

I declare I am full of purpose! I declare God's purpose will prevail in my life. His words, His declarations, His thoughts, His purpose, His plans are greater and will reign superior in my life.

I declare I am exactly what God calls me. He calls me friend. He calls me by my name. He calls me blessed. He calls me His child. He has crowned me with glory and honor. He knows the very number of hairs on my head, and the words on my tongue, before I speak.

I am a chosen child of God and He is a good father. I am new in His sight; old things have passed away. God looks upon me through the lens of love and compassion. When He sees me,

He sees Christ. When He see me, He sees my future, not my past.

I declare that my identify is in Christ. I declare I am the righteousness of God through Christ. I declare I am seated in heavenly places in Christ. I have been adopted into the family of God; I am a Child of God. I am no longer a slave to sin, fear, or my past. I am a child of God.

He picked me! He redeemed me! The eternal God is Abba to me! I declare I am valuable to Him and He cares deeply for me. I declare I will not be discouraged by current situations; my future is bright in Him.

I declare that my pit isn't permanent, and my future isn't pitiful! I declare my now is not my next and my next is big. I declare I will do great exploits because I know my God.

Knowing Him empowers me. My future is utterly secured in Him, and I am safe in His arms. Nothing can separate me from the Love of my Father. I declare what He declares about me. I have a glorious future because He is the author and perfecter of my faith.

Continue Your Declaration Here:

Day 13

"What comes out of our mouth, is a result of what has been allowed to grow in our heart."

Hey Beautiful,

Lies, lies, lies! Oh, the lies people tell us as children. Sticks and stones may break your bones, but words will never hurt you is the biggest lie the people have ever told us. The Bible says that life and death are in the power of our tongue. Our words have the ability to create our reality, to destroy, to curse unfruitful areas in our lives, to move mountains, and to bring walls down. We can dismantle, devour, and destroy with words. We often throw around negative statements, even concerning our own lives, and we don't stop to think about the fruitfulness of those words. Casually saying things like "I feel like I am dying" or "I give up." We must take our words more seriously and be cautious when we fill our atmospheres with negativity!

What comes out of our mouth, is a result of what has been allowed to grow in our heart. That is why we must guard our eye and ear gates, not allowing our heart to get contaminated.

Pray this prayer with me: "Daddy create in me a clean heart and renew the right spirit in me until Your desires become mine and Your thoughts become my faith filled words!"

It is out of the heart, that the mouth speaks. So, for us to adjust our words to match what God says, God must work on our hearts. Many times, when I see someone dismantling their destiny with their words, I can quickly identify that it's a heart condition. Yes, that's a real critical condition and it exist widely among the Christian community. Luke 6:45 (NIV) says, "A good man brings good things out of the good stored up in his heart, and an evil man brings evil things out of the evil stored up in his heart. For the mouth speaks what the heart is full of." And some of us "Christians," are full of... "IT"! Ha! And "It," ain't Jesus!

When your harvest is contaminated, you must evaluate the seed. We can't have a heart full of junk and think that we are going to produce something valuable with our words. We need the great physician to perform a heart transplant on us and give us His heart. We need His heart to do His work. We need His heart to speak His language. We need His heart. Give us Your heart, Father!

When you don't have the heart of the Father, you won't speak the things of the Father. Even after He works on our heart, we still need the Holy Spirit to pray and declare the will of the Father. We don't want to just speak, declare, and decree out of our wicked, immature, emotionally unstable heart, producing Ishmaels. We don't want to produce things out of our flesh, prematurely, out of season, or out of the will of God for our lives.

Understand this my friend, YOUR WORDS WILL PRODUCE...PERIOD. So, what are you producing? What you are producing is a reflection of what has been planted. Our heart soil will produce what we have allowed to be planted and take root. Some of it is so deeply rooted, we need extreme demolition performed. Surface maintenance will not suffice. We need extreme makeovers on our hearts and that, my friend, only God can do for us! See, it is out of a single entity, the heart, one's issues flow. Proverbs 4:23 (NLT) says, "Guard your heart above all else, it determines the course of your life." That sounds real serious, huh? It is just that - serious!

I am going to bless your life real good, right now with the message translation of that scripture which reads, (Proverbs 29: 23-27), "keep vigilant watch over your heart; that's where life start. Don't talk out of both sides of your mouth; avoid careless banter, white lies, and gossip. Keep your eyes straight ahead; ignore all sideshow distraction. Watch your step, and the road will stretch out smooth before you, look neither right nor left; leave evil in the dust."

That is a whole message right there, we can give an offering, say the benediction, close the book and part one from another! Oh, if we could focus right there on that good word! Wow! We need a clean heart to speak this kingdom language; it's a prerequisite! And God gives us that!

I have this beautiful, white shirt that I love so much, (no judgment please, you know you have a shirt or two you would attach the love word to); it was designed just for me. But because I have three boys, I'm always busy, and white and I just ain't friends, I inevitably have to wash it after every wear. But it's okay, because bleach - real bleach, not that off brand stuff, will remove the stains and make it just like new again. Every time! I trust bleach, if bleach did it before, then bleach can do it again.

God is trustworthy with our heart; He can cleanse it over and over and over. But at some point, we have to mature and ask the question - do we want to do what it takes to keep our heart clean, after God does what only he can do? We have a responsibility in this thing. He cleans our heart and then we allow people to draw us into unclean conversation - gossip, careless banter, white lies, etc., and we end up distracted and disheartened in need of that good soap in 1 John 1:9 again!

We can't use our words to bite and devour people and then use them to speak life! You have to make a decision on how you are going to use your words. You won't always get it right, but that is why we have 1 John 1:9 that tells us, 'If we confess our sins, he is faithful and just and will forgive us our sins and purify us from all unrighteousness."

Often, we see Jesus dealing with a person's heart throughout scripture. He was less concerned about what they did and more concerned about why they did it. If we really want to see the things of God manifest in our lives, our hearts cannot be far from him. We can't walk this faith walk, speaking faith talk, with hard, stubborn, unclean hearts. If my words are going to lineup with God, then my will and emotions must line up first.

My prayer as we go into our faith declaration today, is that you take a critical heart check moment. Forgive us, Father, if we have used our powerful words to dismantle anything other than the kingdom of darkness! Create in us a clean heart, so we can speak life.

Scripture Meditation

Proverbs 24:3-4 NIV By wisdom a house is built, and through understanding it is established; through knowledge its rooms are filled with rare and beautiful treasures.

1 Corinthians 13:4-8 NIV Love is patient, love is kind. It does not envy, it does not boast, it is not proud. It does not dishonor others, it is not self-seeking, it is not easily angered, it keeps no record of wrongs. Love does not delight in evil but rejoices with the truth. It always protects, always trusts, always hopes, always perseveres. Love never fails.

Philippians 2:3-7 NIV Do nothing out of selfish ambition or vain conceit. Rather, in humility value others above yourselves, not looking to your own interests but each of you to the interests of the others. In your relationships with one another, have the same mindset as Christ Jesus: Who, being in very nature God, did not consider equality with God something to be used to his own advantage; rather, he made himself nothing by taking the very nature of a servant, being made in human likeness.

Declaration
My Marriage is Blessed

God has healed the wounds in my marriage and blotted out the scars and blemishes. We have been forgiven so freely, and quickly we forgive. I declare we will keep no record of wrongs and release each other quickly of past disappointments and failures. I declare that we are not easily angered or self-seeking. We extend grace in the measure that God extended it to us when He sent His only son to die for our sins. I declare that we seek understanding first, listening to hear and not to speak. We extend immeasurable kindness towards one another all day. Random acts of kindness are our normal. I declare my marriage is full of the love and language of God. We use our words to bless and to build.

Our marriage is blessed and not cursed. I declare we walk as one, in unity and in harmony.

My husband is strong in the Lord and the power of His might. He is led by the Spirit of God. I declare that he is the priest, protector, and provider of our home. I declare he is equipped to lead me. I declare he is full of the Spirit of God. I declare he loves me, as Christ loves the church.

I am a wise woman and I build my home with divine strategy from heaven. I am a supporter and helper to my husband. I declare I cover my home in prayer daily. I declare I am a good thing, a virtuous woman, and my husband has found favor with God. I am a crown to my husband.

I declare we are led by the Spirit of God and another voice, we will not follow. I declare we have sound minds and effective communication. I declare we will listen, answer, and respond with gentleness, turning away wrath. I declare we will listen, answer, and respond with compassion. I declare we will not use our words to bite and devour each other.

I cancel every negative word that has been spoken over our marriage by us and by others. Our marriage is blessed and will bless others. I declare my marriage is an example of God's forgiveness, His love, and His power to refresh, restore, and renew. I declare I submit to Him as he submits to God fully. I declare we operate in the fruit of self-control and through the lens of love.

Our words and deeds are laced in love. We will bring each other good and not harm, all the days of our lives. We are the workmanship of God; therefore, our marriage is His workmanship. It is full of beauty and the glory of God.

I declare my marriage brings honor to God. We are good stewards of all He has given to us; God can trust us with more. He increases us and enlarges our territory. God is our center; faith is our foundation. God is our counselor; the Holy Spirit is our comforter. God is our source, and He supply's all our needs according to His riches in glory.

God is our strength. I declare peace in my marriage! I declare unity in my marriage! We walk in agreement in our spirit. I declare that intimacy in my marriage increases daily! I declare a fire of passion that can't be quenched but burns forever for my spouse alone. I declare a healthy desire for one another and not someone outside our covenant. I declare we are faithful and trustworthy. I declare that we are abiding in truth and seeking understanding daily. I declare effective communication in my marriage and in my home! I declare fruitfulness in my marriage!

Our seeds are blessed! We are generational curse breakers, legacy builders, and Kingdom financiers. We are builders and we support one another's God given dreams and endeavors. We are a Kingdom couple and we operate in Kingdom principles and we get Kingdom results!

Continue Your Declaration Here:

Day 14

"There is no longer an option to speak contrary to the word of God concerning you!"

Hey Beautiful,

You made it to day 14, but it's not over! Far from over! We are mastering speaking the language of heaven, and I know how difficult this can be. We have been using our words for years to destroy and delay what God has for us, to devour and dismantle our purpose! But, now we are using the language of success, the very language of heaven. We are becoming familiar and comfortable with speaking like Jesus, our greatest example.

He curses fig trees with His words, and we can likewise curse unproductive, unfruitful areas of our lives at the root, with our words. He calls dead things to come forth with His words. Likewise, we can raise every Lazarus in our lives with our faith language! He created and formed the world with His words...what are you desiring to create today?

What do you want to see manifest? The power is in your tongue! Don't you allow the enemy to tell you this doesn't work; be committed! Be committed to speaking differently (you saw the fruit of your old language). What do you have to lose? Be committed to declaring life and prosperity to everything that is attached to you.

I love that song by Jekalyn Carr, that declares "Everything attached to me wins." Let that be the language and stance that you take today! Be committed to declaring victory! Be committed to cursing and declaring death to everything tormenting you! You can do this my friend!

I speak the supernatural strength of our Creator to saturate you now, as you continue to SPEAK LIFE. Why do you need strength? Because I know our adversary, and he will try, if he hasn't already, to weaken your confession through discouragement and weariness. But you shall speak!

You shall declare and decree! And you shall see exactly what you say! There is no longer an option to speak contrary to the word of God concerning you! Faith talk is how our Father requires us to operate. The bible says the just shall live by faith! Just...justified - that's us. I know how hard this faith talk can be but it's worth it to push through and keep speaking.

Faith is totally about speaking those things we don't see, until we do see them. Faith is speaking what you expect, not what you're experiencing. Faith is speaking out of His Word and not out of your limited understanding. It's not easy, but it is becoming your lifestyle.

Let me have a moment of transparency. I had one foot in and one foot out of this life of faith for many years, before God firmed my footing in it. Let me save you years of double-minded behavior and wavering confessions. If you live in the presence of God, it will be impossible to speak things outside His will. It will be difficult and feel unnatural to speak against His will for your life. It's in His presence that we receive refreshing and strength for our faith walk.

We receive the supernatural strength and empowerment of God to speak out the things of God. It is only when you live in the presence of God, you are able to speak a Word over your own life and shift the atmosphere. I had a different declaration that I wanted to end this Food for Faith Declaration Manual with, but the Holy Spirit instructed me to end it with a declaration that will help you enter into His presence and live there every day.

The precious blood of our High Priest has made the presence of God accessible for us! We have access to live there! Nothing is stopping us from entering His presence each and every day. We can live there. Glory! He wants us there.

I speak prophetically in your life and declare that you shall live in the presence of God. You will always make room for Him. I speak an undying hunger and thirst for His presence over you! Only He will be able to satisfy your soul.

I declare that you will press into His presence daily, so that the words you speak over your life are released from a place of power and authority. I cancel every attack on your spiritual voice! The enemy will not silence you. You will speak up! You will speak out! You shall decree and declare! You are full of power and authority and you will operate in the fullness of God! You shall prophesy over your own life and see the manifestation of it! Your voice shakes the camp of the enemy! Your faith filled words release healing and restoration! Speak! Speak life! Heaven is backing you. Speak! Angels are being deployed, Speak!

Scripture Meditation:

Psalm 21:6 NIV Surely you have granted him unending blessings and made him glad, with the joy of your presence.

Psalm 114:7-8 BSB Tremble, O earth, at the presence of the Lord, at the presence of the God of Jacob, who turned the rock into a pool, the flint into a fountain of water.

Psalm 84:10 NIV Better is one day in your courts than a thousand elsewhere; I would rather be a doorkeeper in the house of my God than dwell in the tents of the wicked.

Hebrews 10:19-20 BSB Therefore, brothers, since we have confidence to enter the holy places by the blood of Jesus, by the new and living way that he opened for us through the curtain, that is, through his flesh.

Psalm 42:1-2 KJV As the hart panteth after the water brooks, so panteth my soul after thee, O God. My soul thirsteth for God, for the living of God; when shall I come and appear before God?

Isaiah 6:1-5 BSB In the year that King Uzziah died, I saw the Lord seated on a throne, high and exalted; and the train of His robe filled the temple. Above Him stood seraphim, each having six wings: With two wings they covered their faces, with two they covered their feet, and with two they were flying. And they called out to one another: Holy, holy, holy is the LORD of Hosts; His glory fills all the earth. The doorposts and thresholds shook at the sound of their voices, and the temple was filled with smoke. Then I said, "Woe is me, for I am ruined, because I am a man of unclean lips dwelling among a people of unclean lips, and my eyes have seen the King, the LORD of Hosts.

Declaration
I Will Live in His Presence

I declare that I will live in the presence of God. I will dwell there! I will reside there! I am free there! Nothing can keep me from the presence of God. I declare there is no veil restraining me and I will not allow a veil to be placed between me and His presence.

My perfect sacrifice, my High Priest, gives me access to the ineffable Holy God. I have access! I can enter in! I will enter in! There is no other place I desire to be. I desire more of You God and less of me. I desire to feel Your manifested presence. I declare the weight of Your Glory is resting on me now. I cry out like Moses for Your glory, show me Your Glory. I declare that I will see the glory of the Lord today. I will experience

You in a fresh, new way.

I want to see Your face! I declare Your face, I will seek. I desire to gaze upon the beauty of Your holiness. I bow down and worship, consume me. I declare that there is nothing I thirst for more, than you. Cause me to hunger after you! Nothing shall be able to satisfy my thirst but you.

Overwhelm me with Your presence. Make me aware of You in this moment. I declare there are no distractions that can keep me from You. I make time for You. I make room for You. I come to your feet. I declare I will remain at Your feet, pouring until I am completely empty, and you refill me. I declare nothing will compete with my time with You because You are my first priority.

I declare my flesh will not win! My flesh will not dominate! My flesh will not keep me out of Your presence. I declare sin shall not keep me separated. You dealt with my sin issue and I am free to be in Your presence. The blood of Jesus covers me. The blood of Jesus qualifies me. The blood of Jesus removed the veil. I declare, I am in the presence of God!

I am standing on Holy Ground. Tremble Earth, for the presence of the Lord is here! My soul pants after thee, oh God and You alone! I declare His presence is refreshing me! I declare His presence is refilling me! I declare His presence is changing me! I declare His presence is protecting me! I declare His presence is strengthening me! I declare His presence is exposing me - woe is me! I declare His presence is purging me! I declare His presence is molding me.

I submit and release all of me in Your Holy presence. The King of Glory is filling my space, filling my atmosphere, filling me. I declare the presence of God is inescapable to me. I am an addict, completely addicted to Your presence. I can't breathe without you. I can't live without you. I can't move without you!

I will not live or move outside of Your presence. In Your presence, I am free! Blessed our those who dwell in Your house, in Your courts, and in Your presence! I declare I am blessed because I am in Your presence. Restrain me here! Arrest me here! Keep me here! Don't let me go! Don't release me!

Continue Your Declaration Here:

ABOUT THE AUTHOR

Candice is a Speaker/Preacher/Elevation Coach Empowering and Educating Women in Ministry and Business to elevate to excellence!

Candice has been blessed with a creative ability to effectively communicate the gospel of the Lord Jesus Christ. Her ministry transcends denominational, social, and racial barriers. She is committed to expanding the Kingdom of God on earth through effectively empowering, equipping, and evangelizing.

Candice has a passion for developing Gods people and bringing more souls to the Kingdom of God through preaching and teaching under the anointing of the Holy Spirit. She gave her life to Christ as a young child, and knew as a child she was called into Ministry to preach the gospel! She loves the Lord her God with all of her heart, soul, and might.

Candice has been married to Linston Jones III since 2002. They are the proud parents of three boys (Linston, Cameron, and Carsten) and she believes that God gives great gifts we call children. They currently reside in Kennesaw, GA. She is the Daughter of Marietta Verges and National Evangelist, Pastor Dennis K Hutchins of Orlando, FL.

Candice is a Graduate of Baker College of Flint with an Associate's Degree in Business Administration, a Graduate of Agape Faith Bible Training Center in Birch Run, MI. and a Graduate of Liberty University in Lynchburg, VA.

Candice has been teaching and serving in the Church of God from childhood, and preaching as an ordained Minister since 2011.

She has served Leadership and served as a Youth Leader, Teacher, Minister, Administrator and Coordinator for New

Harvest Church in Flint, MI and other organizations. She is consistently successful in developing innovative strategies to improve teamwork and productivity; has proven ability to communicate effectively with individuals on all levels.

Candice is gifted to teach, train, and motivate others. She has effective leadership and team building skills. She believes it absolutely takes teamwork to make a dream work and is known for developing dream teams.

Candice is a professional retail leader, working as an Area Manager, Store manager, and Field Trainer for over 16 years. She has developed extraordinary leaders, built dream teams, and elevated talent and client service in many locations. She has the ability to effectively connect and communicate with a diversity of people.

She is simply a lover of God and His people and committed to helping people speak life every day, utilizing the power and authority of every believer.